TO VET SCHOOL AND BEYOND

TO VET SCHOOL AND BEYOND

A GUIDE FOR YOUNG, ASPIRING VETS

LORNA CLARK

Books

First published 2021

Copyright © Lorna Clark 2021

All rights reserved. No part of this publication may be reproduced, stored in a retrieval system, or transmitted, in any form or by any means, electronic, mechanical, photocopying, recording or otherwise, without prior permission of the copyright holder.

Published by
5M Books Ltd,
Lings, Great Easton,
Essex CM6 2HH, UK,
Tel: +44 (0)330 1333 580
www.5mbooks.com

A Catalogue record for this book is available from the British Library

ISBN 9781789180916
eISBN 9781789181906
DOI 10.52517.9781789181906

Cover, internal design and initial layouts by James Powell
Additional design and layouts by Clive Holloway
Printed by Hobbs The Printers Ltd, Totton, Hampshire
Photos by author unless acknowledged otherwise

CONTENTS

1	SO YOU THINK YOU WANT TO BE A VET?	1
2	HOW BEING A VET HAS CHANGED	13
3	THINGS TO CONSIDER – THE GOOD, THE BAD AND THE MEDIOCRE	21
4	TO VET SCHOOL	27
5	AND BEYOND	59
	BEING A SMALL ANIMAL VET	60
	BEING A CHARITY VET	66
	BEING AN EMERGENCY VET	69
	BEING A REFERRAL VET	73
	BEING AN EQUINE VET	77
	BEING A FARM ANIMAL VET	80
	BEING A LOCUM VET	83
	BEING A POULTRY VET	85
	BEING A ZOO VET	88
	BEING A FISH VET	92
	BEING A RESEARCH VET	95
	BEING A VET IN EDUCATION	97
	BEING A VET IN INDUSTRY	99
	BEING A VET IN AFRICA	102
	BEING A GOVERNMENT VETERINARY OFFICER	104
6	MEMORABLE AND INTERESTING CASES	107
7	REACH FOR THE STARS	121

My friend Heather,
who loved being a vet

1. SO YOU THINK YOU WANT TO BE A VET?

> **I'M LORNA, AND I'M A VET. WHAT IMAGE DOES THAT MAKE YOU THINK OF?**

That time in the zoo...

Fun times on the farm!?

Walter and his new wheels!!

> **I THOUGHT SO...**
>
> It's what people often think of when I explain to them that I'm a vet, but actually my job as a veterinary surgeon and more importantly, my qualification, allows me to do a whole host of things.

HERE IS WHAT SOME OF MY COLLEAGUES WORKING IN THE DIFFERENT AREAS OF THE PROFESSION DO...

Some work with pet or companion animals

Some work for the government or veterinary charities

Some are involved with teaching

Some work in zoos or aquariums, or even with wildlife

Some work in the veterinary industry, maybe for a pet food or a pharmaceutical (drug) company

And some work with other unusual species such as fish or birds

THE AIM OF THIS BOOK IS TO GIVE YOU A BETTER IDEA OF WHAT THE JOB OF A VETERINARY SURGEON INVOLVES

Times have changed since there was little more choice than to join a farm or pet animal practice – there are now a whole host of exciting career opportunities for those who think that being a vet might be the job for them.

In this book we will explore what being a vet is really like – the good things and the not so good things about the job, what it is like to be a vet now, and how that has changed from how it used to be.

We will think about the things that you need to do now, and over the next few years if you would like to be a vet, and delve a bit deeper into what it is like to study veterinary medicine at university.

Finally, we will look a bit closer at the various career opportunities and roles available after graduation – the day when you finally become a vet.

But first things first:

- Are you an animal lover, deeply committed to looking after animals and protecting their welfare?

- Are you prepared to study hard to gain qualifications and commit to completing additional work experience enabling you to reach the entry requirements of the Veterinary degree course?

- Can you communicate well, and do you enjoy working with people?

IF YOU ANSWERED 'YES' TO THE THREE QUESTIONS ABOVE, THEN READ ON...

Whenever someone talks about wanting to be a vet, one of the first things people will say is 'that's a really difficult thing to do' or 'isn't it harder to become a vet than a doctor?'.

Although people mean well, these comments can discourage people from entering the profession as they may be put off by the challenges ahead of them.

Getting through the selection process to get into vet school and completing the course is a **HUGE** achievement, but it is certainly possible, particularly with thought and preparation – starting **NOW!**

Several veterinary schools exist in the UK, each offering over 100 places (and at the moment this number is rapidly increasing), and there are many more places to study if you take into account vet schools in other countries.

All you need is to get **ONE** place at any **ONE** of the vet schools, and your career goal is within reach.

THAT SOUNDS A BIT MORE PROMISING, DOESN'T IT?

Get prepared and start early to ensure that you fulfil the entry requirements, and there is no reason why a place at vet school isn't for **YOU**.

When you qualify as a vet in the UK, you are eligible to become a Member of the Royal College of Veterinary Surgeons, and use the letters MRCVS after your name.

The Royal College of Veterinary Surgeons (RCVS) was established in 1844 when a Royal Charter was granted, recognizing the 'veterinary art' as a profession and ensuring that those practising it were suitably trained and qualified.

Before that, farriers or blacksmiths (people who made and fitted horseshoes on horses) were considered 'horse-doctors', as from their work they had a very basic knowledge of equine (horse) disease and, as there were no regulations regarding the treatment of animals at this time, anyone else could turn their hand to treating an animal too, if they fancied it.

Following the establishment of the RCVS, the first Veterinary Surgeons Act was passed in 1881 and a register of veterinary surgeons was established, which meant that the treating of animals was regulated, and restricted to certain, properly authorized people.

Over 150 years on, it is still necessary to be a member of the College in order to legally practice as a vet in the UK.

To be a vet you need a specific qualification – a university degree in veterinary medicine which usually requires five years of study. That sounds like a long time, but there is a lot to learn, and it goes quite fast!

One of the things that I really enjoyed about studying veterinary medicine was the variety of learning.

The first two years are spent mainly learning anatomy, physiology and animal science and becoming familiar with animal handling and animal management, and then the final three years are focused on building on that knowledge, and learning about pathology (the cause and effect of disease), how to make a diagnosis and treatment, and applying it to becoming a vet.

Usually, the last year of vet school is lecture-free, and spent on work placements, usually in veterinary practices or other veterinary establishments.

These placements are called 'rotations' and provide a really practical learning experience. I think this is the year that I enjoyed the most when I was at vet school – it really felt like becoming a vet was just around the corner.

Vet school was a long time ago now for me, so I met up with Katie Macauley who is a vet student in her third year, to find out what learning to be a vet is like for her.

HELLO! MY NAME IS Katie

I live in Surrey and I'm in my third year of study at the vet school there. I have one dog – a red Labrador called Alfie who eats absolutely anything and everything! I am a very active person and when I am not at college or working – I love running, cycling and horse-riding.

Wow! You sound like a very busy and motivated person. Did you always want to be a vet?

Yes, I have always wanted to be a vet, from as long as I can remember. I think I've been really lucky, knowing what I've wanted to do – as I've always had a goal to work towards. It's been really helpful through school, having something to keep me focused.

So, how did you get on in your GSCEs and A levels?

I got 11 GCSEs, including all of the sciences, English and maths, and then geography and French, because those were two subjects that I really enjoyed. I also got four A levels in biology, chemistry, physics and home economics.

That's brilliant!
What work experience did you do in preparation for applying to school?

Lambing and calving are both really good fun and you often get to do lots of 'hands-on' things like delivering lambs and calves, and administering medicines. I spent a week at a canine hydrotherapy centre where I learnt about and got to do some dog massage, which was pretty cool!

I enjoyed spending time in vet practices too – watching what a vet does day to day is a great way to see whether it might be the right job for you. If you don't have time to do more experience than the vet schools require it doesn't matter. The key really is quality over quantity. A few weeks where you learn a lot is much more worthwhile than spending a year somewhere where you don't learn anything.

That's really good to know. Can you tell me a bit more about the university application process?

I applied to vet school in October 2015. The first part of the journey is writing your personal statement, which is basically just a piece of writing about yourself, including why you would make a good vet, and what strengths and good qualities you have. In the UK you apply through an organization called UCAS. You do this online and it is pretty simple: it just involves a lot of filling in details and exam grades and then selecting your universities and keeping your fingers crossed until you hear back.

Your application was obviously successful then?

Yes. I got two interviews, one at Liverpool and one at Surrey. Both were MMIs (multiple mini interviews), where you don't just sit in front of a panel of people and talk to them, you move around the room and sit at different tables for 5 minutes each, answering one interview question at each table.

All of the universities have slightly different interview processes so it is well worth reading up beforehand so you are prepared for each. Most of them involve an interview aspect, where you chat a bit about why you want to be a vet, your opinions on vet issues, and maybe interesting cases you have seen, and some include practical parts like group discussions, skills like building a Lego® model, and simple maths calculations.

The university then get in contact with you within a few days or weeks to let you know their decision, and you can then decide which offer to accept and which university you want to go to. I got one offer, from Surrey, which I was very happy to accept!

That's really interesting – who'd have thought you'd build Lego® at a vet school interview! It's great news when you get a place – as it can be quite difficult to get in. Do you have any advice for the readers of this book on applying to vet school?

 It felt amazing to receive the offer! My advice would be – don't be disheartened if you don't get in the first time! Lots and lots of people at vet school have applied two or three times before – some have done different courses beforehand, some take gap years, and there is absolutely nothing wrong with that at all.

Veterinary medicine is a tough and competitive degree to get a place on, and just because you get rejected one year does not mean you aren't good enough! So, don't give up, reapply and you never know!

Good advice! What are the bits that you most enjoy about being a vet student?

 I feel really lucky to be a vet student, and it is a lot of fun. I find the work really enjoyable and I have met some wonderful people, both friends at university, and vets and vet nurses while out on placements. It opens so many opportunities for you to get involved in different things no matter what field you are interested in. Some of the best parts are the practical bits, like animal handling, which at Surrey starts right at the beginning of the course, as well as getting to have a go at clinical skills like suturing, scrubbing-up for surgery and working through cases, because those are the parts that really make you feel like a vet.

And what are the least positive aspects – the things you find the most difficult or stressful?

 Being a vet student is intense and you won't love it all the time. It is a long course and sometimes it can feel like it is never-ending or that the things you are learning aren't going to be useful in the future, but there is always something that will pick you up and remind you why you are there in the first place.

Most of our university holidays are taken up working in practices on placement, which can be really tiring and annoying, especially if you have non-vet friends who have a lot more time off than you do.

Sometimes, you feel like you don't know much and can't do anything, but it is important not to forget that you are there to learn and aren't expected to do everything right straightaway.

Finding the right revision strategy is also difficult, because what worked in school might not work at university due to the amount of work you have to do. However, there are lots of resources available to help.

So, what's been your favourite bit so far, and what are you looking forward to in the future on your course?

My favourite bit was probably scrubbing into my first surgery while I was on placement, because after all of the hard work and long hours I had been putting in at university, it made me feel like I was one step closer to my goal of becoming a vet! I can't wait for the fifth year, where I don't have any lectures at all. I spend the year in practices and get to take on my own cases and put all of my skills and knowledge into practice to make animals better.

Sounds exciting! I must say, I really enjoyed my final year. It really felt like you were almost there! On another note – what would you say are the three most important skills you use being a vet student?

The ability to laugh, both at life and at yourself, is really so important, especially for vet students. It is a long journey to become a vet and it isn't easy for anyone, with lots of exams to pass, skills to develop and information to understand. Even when you have graduated, it doesn't get much easier, with long hours and hard situations to deal with. You won't always get things right all of the time; every vet makes mistakes and we all have our fair share of embarrassing stories about situations we've been in, where we've been kicked or scratched or soaked in blood, cow poo or something equally disgusting, but being able to have a laugh when these things happen makes you so much happier.

The ability to motivate yourself to work is also really important because university isn't like school where it is very structured and you have someone telling you what work to do and when – all of that now comes from you.

Communication skills with people from all walks of life are also so important. We are in a very important position to advise people about making the best decisions for their animals, and discussing difficult topics like euthanasia, so being able to communicate clearly and compassionately with people is something any vet should be able to do.

Can you describe a typical day at vet school?

Usually I get up around 7am, have a good breakfast and get ready. A typical day at vet school is 9am to 4pm, with three hours of lectures in the morning, an hour for lunch and then two to three hours of practical classes in the afternoon, which are usually all on the same topic to help you put the information you learn in the morning into practice.

Practical classes are either in the laboratories with dead animal tissue to work with, learning anatomy or pathology, practising clinical skills like suturing or injecting, or examining the live animals we have on site, which are always my favourites! Wednesday afternoons are kept free every week for sports and general chill-out time. I am usually home by 5 or 6pm, then go for a run, and then have dinner. Some evenings I will write up lectures or do some revision, and others I like to spend watching TV before heading to bed, because it is really important to let your brain have a rest!

So, what other things do you get involved with at university apart from studying?

While it is true that you have a lot of work to do, it is so important to have hobbies alongside vet school so you have good work–life balance. In my first year, I was a member of the veterinary society, which ran events like trampolining, ice skating and pub quizzes, which were all great ways to make friends and get to know the area.

 I also had a membership to the sports centre that Surrey University has, with all sorts of options from climbing, a gym, a swimming pool, tennis courts, horse-riding – you name it, they have it! There are also loads of non-sporting clubs so there is pretty much something for everyone! The university also run all sorts of interesting talks covering a range of topics like wildlife rescue and animal first aid, which I love to go to (plus the free cake and pizza you get are always a bonus!!).

Sounds brilliant! Lastly, will you just finish this sentence off for me. I really want to be a vet because …

 I want to be able to make a difference to people's and animals' lives – and this is a job where I feel I can make an impact!

Thanks Katie. It's been great chatting to you! Good luck with the rest of your studies!

2. HOW BEING A VET HAS CHANGED

ANIMALS ARE ALL AROUND US, AND NO MATTER HOW BIG OR SMALL, ANIMALS NEED VETS TO HELP KEEP THEM FIT AND HEALTHY, OR TO HELP THEM WHEN THEY ARE ILL. MANY OF US PICTURE A VET WEARING A **STETHOSCOPE** AROUND THEIR NECK, GOING OUT ON VISITS TO SEE **FARM ANIMALS** AND THEN HEADING BACK TO THE PRACTICE TO LOOK AFTER SOME **CATS** OR **DOGS**. BUT OFTEN THAT'S NO LONGER THE CASE - AND THERE ARE SEVERAL REASONS WHY. TO UNDERSTAND WHAT IT IS LIKE BEING A VET TODAY, WE NEED TO UNDERSTAND A BIT MORE ABOUT HOW OUR RELATIONSHIP WITH ANIMALS HAS CHANGED OVER TIME.

OVER THE LAST 50-60 YEARS PET OWNERSHIP HAS INCREASED TREMENDOUSLY, AND IT IS THOUGHT THAT RIGHT NOW, NEARLY 50 PER CENT OF ADULTS IN THE UK OWN PETS.

A special report from one of the leading pet charities, estimates that in 2021 there were 10.7 million pet cats, 9.6 million pet dogs and 900,000 pet rabbits in the UK – that's **A LOT** of animals that need looking after – and doesn't include all other animals, like farm animals, zoo animals and animals that live in the wild.

The most common pets are dogs and cats, although rabbits and small rodents, such as guinea pigs, hamsters and gerbils, are also popular. Exotic pets are also kept – like certain reptiles, tortoises and tropical fish. Horse ownership is on the increase too, and things like horse-racing and show-jumping generate huge public interest and have whole industries built around them.

FARMING IS CHANGING TOO.
FOOD PRODUCTION HAS HAD TO INCREASE ENORMOUSLY TO MEET GLOBAL DEMAND AND FEED THE EVER-INCREASING HUMAN POPULATION.

Farmers often farm intensively and supply in large volumes to wholesale suppliers or supermarkets, who then sell the product on to their customers. As a result, we have 'intensive farming', which is raising farm animals for meat or produce on a large scale. At the other end of the scale, some farmers have gone back to producing small quantities of home-reared produce, sometimes organically farmed or from rare breeds, as some people like to buy meat and farm produce that has been reared on a smaller and less intensive scale.

Regardless of the way any animal is raised or kept, it is the role of the veterinary surgeon to safeguard their health and welfare and work with owners, farmers or keepers to ensure that we do the utmost to protect and help the animals under our care.

All these animals still need vets to look after them, though our role and the way we look after them has changed significantly. There are now less 'mixed practices' (the term we use to describe a veterinary practice that looks after both pet animals and/or farm animals and/or horses) and there are fewer vets who treat more than one type of animal – be that pets, farm animals, horses or other types of animals or species. The veterinary profession has evolved over the years in a number of ways, and we shall now look at some of them a bit closer.

PATIENT OR POPULATION HEALTH?

In pet animal and horse practices the vets are mainly focused on treating their patients as individual animals and getting the best treatment and outcome for them – a bit like a person going to see a doctor, whereas farm animal vets tend to think about animals in larger numbers – as herds or flocks – and the overall health of the group of animals as a whole. Looking after groups of animals, rather than each one individually – and maximizing the production of these animals – be it milk, meat or eggs is given the term 'population medicine' or 'herd/flock health'. Treating individual animals compared to whole flocks or herds is quite different, and vets more commonly now choose to go with one or the other – hence choose small animal, horse OR farm practice, rather than do both.

However, although we think about heard health being something that a large animal or farm vet would do, population medicine can still be applied to small animal practice in some scenarios – for example, looking after lots of cats in a cattery, or lots of dogs at a charity rehoming centre. And similarly, although farm vets often practice population medicine – they still treat individual patients – for example doing a Caesarean section on a cow (an operation where a large cut is made in the body wall and uterus of the cow to facilitate removal of a calf, which is quite a common operation in farm animal practice and is done for several different reasons).

KNOWING IT ALL

As veterinary medicine has advanced over the years, and our knowledge has increased, there is more and more to learn and more things that we can do for each individual species of animal. Therefore, practices and vets nowadays usually become more focused on a particular type of animal. While at vet school, you are taught about all species, but you soon realize that even after you graduate, there is a lot more to learn about each and every one!

ONE SIZE NO LONGER FITS ALL

Back in the old days, veterinary practices wouldn't have anywhere near the types or range of equipment that we have today. In my practice we have an X-ray machine for taking radiographs, a special machine for processing the radiographs we have taken so that we can see a picture, an ultrasound machine, a microscope and a dental machine – as well as lots of other equipment for administering anaesthetics and cleaning our surgical kits. Different equipment is needed for different types of veterinary practice. An X-ray machine for a cat and dog is quite different to the type you would need to take an X-ray of a horse. This equipment is very expensive, and often quite big – so if you want your veterinary practice to see lots of different species of animal, you'd need to invest quite a lot of money and it would have to be a very big place! Many large mixed practices are often spread over several different sites. This is another reason why there are fewer practices now which have all the facilities to treat both small and large animals.

SPECIALISTS AND REFERRAL CENTRES

Advances in veterinary medicine and technology has enabled cutting-edge procedures and advanced techniques to become available, which often require a degree of specialization. This has led to specialist veterinary hospitals being set up. Animals can be referred from a local or 'first opinion' veterinary practice to specialist centres that have the facilities, equipment and expertise to deal with more complex and difficult cases – a bit like going to your local doctor, and then being sent to the hospital for further tests and treatment. Referral centres have lots of specialist staff and equipment and are therefore ideally suited to treating more complicated and difficult to diagnose cases.

DO YOU HAVE ANY SPECIALIST REFERRAL CENTRES NEAR WHERE YOU LIVE? IF SO, FIND OUT WHAT THEY DO.

INDEPENDENT VERSUS CORPORATE VETERINARY PRACTICES

One of the biggest changes to the veterinary profession has been the loss of smaller, privately owned (or independent) veterinary practices and the growth of large veterinary corporate practices, as a result of changes to regulations which now enable veterinary practices to be owned and run by people who aren't vets.

Historically, veterinary practices were owned by vets, and a typical career path involved becoming an assistant vet after graduation and working at a practice, in the hope that at some point you would be able to buy a share in the business and become a practice owner. These types of practices are classed as independent. The owners of the practice work there, and are in charge of running the practice and organizing the day-to-day activities.

Nowadays, many of these practices have been bought and are operated by private companies – these are termed corporate practices, and this type of veterinary practice is becoming more and more common.

So, what's the difference?
Hopefully, not much! Ultimately, we are all offering a similar service and trying to achieve the same thing. Unfortunately, the rise of corporate owned practices has meant that there are less opportunities for new vets to buy into a practice and become a practice owner – but on the flip side, there is still nothing stopping you setting up on your own as an independent practice – which is what I have done.

There will be differences in working for an independent or a corporate veterinary practice but essentially, whichever type of practice you work for, you are still a vet. Some people argue that smaller, independent practices can provide a better and more personal service, and corporate practices, as they are run by business people, are better organized and offer more opportunities for promotion without the stress or financial burden of practice ownership. But this is very much a generalization and wouldn't be true of all practices.

Whatever your preference, the corporate ownership model is here to stay, and while there are pros and cons to both types of practice, there is no reason that in the future good corporate and good independent practices will not continue to exist alongside each other.

LET'S HEAR IT FOR THE GIRLS!

One thing that is very noticeable is the increasing number of women who work in the profession. Times have changed, and female vets now outnumber male vets – and there are far more female students than male students at vet school. Being a vet is a great career opportunity for both men and women, and as working patterns change to enable greater work flexibility and, with the diverse range of roles available, working as a vet, whether you are male or female, can be made to fit quite nicely around family life.

Aleen Isobel Cust was the first female veterinary surgeon to be recognized by the RCVS in 1924. She actually finished her degree in 1900 and won the gold medal for zoology, but she wasn't allowed to sit her exams, as back then the RCVS only accepted male students as members. A special act was eventually passed that meant that Aleen was able to be officially recognized as a veterinary surgeon, and when she died in 1937 there were 60 female vets recognized by the profession and the number has been slowly increasing ever since.

EMERGENCY!

One big difference, even since I left vet school, is the reduction in the number of veterinary practices that do their own 'out of hours' (OOH) or emergency care. Veterinary practices have a duty of care to their patients to ensure that they can access veterinary services in the case of an emergency outside of the practice opening hours. In other words, a practice has to have a vet available 24 hours a day, 7 days a week, 365 days a year.

It used to be that vets would share the OOH rota – with each vet taking it in turns to be on duty to respond to emergency calls overnight or at weekends. This could be quite stressful and the workload very variable. It was also very frustrating to sometimes be woken at night or called in to work at the weekend, when it was something that could actually wait to be seen the next working day. The service provided by practices was also variable – from having a full team at a practice overnight with a nurse staying to give patient care, to seeing a vet, on their own, who had just got out of bed! Not great for anyone concerned!

What we have seen over the last decade in small animal practice, is the emergence of veterinary services that have been set up to deal exclusively with the overnight and weekend cases of their member practices. Any small animal practice can join up to a local emergency service provider, and when the practice closes at night, the phones are transferred to the emergency vets, who are fully staffed with a team of people, ready to deal with cases with the same level of service and efficiency that would be experienced during a normal working day. The customer might have to go to a different place with their pet when their usual practice is closed – but once their vets is open again they are transferred back for ongoing care.

These emergency veterinary services make life much nicer for small animal vets – the vast majority of whom can go home at night and not have to worry about being called back out overnight or at weekends, and patients are given a much better level of care. These services can be quite expensive for owners, but this reflects the anti-social hours covered and the quality of care on offer.

Unfortunately, these services are only really available, at the moment, to small animal practices. Vets working with farm animals or horses generally still have to take part in a traditional OOH rota.

3. THINGS TO CONSIDER – THE GOOD, THE BAD AND THE MEDIOCRE

We've already discussed that becoming a vet takes a **LONG TIME** and **LOTS OF STUDY**, as well as a significant amount of your own free time spent gaining work experience, which is often unpaid. And after all that, when you become a vet, it can be quite different from how you expected the job to be. So, with what you've read about so far, do you still want to be a vet?

IF THE ANSWER IS YES!
THEN TURN TO THE NEXT PAGE

GREAT! LET'S TAKE A CLOSER LOOK AT THE JOB AND SOME OF THE GOOD BITS AND THE NOT SO GOOD BITS - IT WILL HOPEFULLY GIVE YOU PLENTY TO THINK ABOUT AND HELP YOU DECIDE IF YOU STILL THINK THAT BEING A VET IS THE RIGHT JOB FOR YOU!

People think that being a vet is about working with animals. Which it is – but it is also about working with people. Do you like speaking to people?

Can you imagine yourself standing at a consultation room table examining a pet and chatting to the owners or discussing a pet's progress or laboratory results over the phone? Can you imagine yourself having a discussion with a farmer as to how he/she can improve the health or welfare of their herd of cows?

Being a vet can be stressful. We don't just make things better and save lives – sometimes we also have to deal with death and sad, worried or frustrated owners. It's important to think about whether you could manage the day-to-day stresses and strains of the job, and if you have the right skills to deal with difficult situations. A keyword here is 'resilience', something that we will hear a bit more about later on.

Good day!

Bad day...

Friday!!

MEANWHILE, LETS LOOK AT SOME OF THE GOOD STUFF AND THE NOT SO GOOD STUFF TO CONSIDER...

Crossed wires

Being a vet can be daunting. There is so much to learn at university, and there is still more to learn after you graduate. Animals can't talk – so they can't tell you how they feel, and sometimes it can be difficult to find out what is wrong.

Sometimes we don't know exactly what is wrong, and we have to make decisions based on the information available to us at the time, and have the confidence to use our own judgement when considering the right course of action.

Making an animal better and keeping them healthy gives you a great feeling. Being a vet is often a very satisfying job to do and there are lots of bits that are very rewarding. Helping people who are sad or worried about their pet and helping them get through a difficult time can be immensely satisfying.

Being a vet means that often no two days are the same. This makes your working life interesting and often makes the working day go very quickly! Being a vet is certainly not boring!

However, unpredictable days at work may also mean that you don't always finish on time and may end up working longer hours than you expect. Some vets will also still be expected to take part in an 'out of hours' rota – so in addition to working during the week, you may also be working at night or at the weekend.

Achieving a degree in veterinary medicine is not easy – it involves many years of study, but it is a widely recognized and respected qualification. This means that when you graduate you have a really good knowledge and skill base that can be used not only to be a vet, but also to do other jobs if you decide to explore career opportunities outside the profession.

Graduation Day

When you qualify as a vet, you can treat all types of animals and you are also able to practice basic medical and surgical techniques without any further qualification. Some vets go on to do further studies to improve their knowledge, or they may choose to specialize, but additional qualifications aren't essential to be a practising vet. This is different to being a doctor, where obtaining a degree in medicine is very much just the start of your career, and further qualifications are necessary to enable you to undertake work in a certain area.

Much of the day-to-day work of a first opinion vet in general practice can be fairly routine. Although no two days are the same, routine procedures and preventive medicine or dealing with common types of disease can take up quite a lot of our time most days, as well as dealing with paperwork.

For most vets, the day-to-day work becomes routine and the real challenges and exciting cases can be few and far between. For some people, after all that challenge and hard work at vet school, they can find life in general practice boring or frustrating.

The average salary for a newly qualified vet in the UK in 2021 is £30,000. The employment rate following graduation is very high for vets and the starting salary is relatively competitive for professionals. However, salary rises are often smaller and go up slower than in other jobs or career paths, and some people feel frustrated as they earn less than other professional people.

Paperwork!!!

Though further qualifications, or promotion to veterinary management, or opening your own veterinary practice or business are all possibilities that can significantly increase your earning potential.

In practice, providing your services as a veterinary surgeon comes at a financial cost to the owner – and in addition there will be drugs and investigations to pay for. As well as treating the animal, discussions with owners about the costs involved can be challenging, and financial limitations may alter what you can do for a patient and the type of treatment that you can provide.

This can mean that you can't always do what you would like to do, or what you have been taught to do at vet school.

In some ways this can be frustrating and depressing, especially if the outcome of a case isn't good, but the challenge of tailoring what you can do with the finances available can really test your problem-solving skills and can result in some great job satisfaction.

Being a vet can sometimes test your patience and your beliefs. Not only are we trying to do our best to promote good animal welfare standards, but we also have to respect other people's opinions and values. Sometimes in our job it is necessary to compromise, or have potentially difficult conversations with people.

Also, don't forget a career as a vet is not just about working with cute puppies and kittens, we come across many tricky situations in our job that can be stressful to deal with and require a great deal of thought.

For example, an owner has a dog with very bad hip joints which means that it is likely to encounter lots of health problems throughout its life, but worse still, it is likely to pass these issues on to any puppies it has. We advise the owner NOT to breed from the dog, but the owner refuses to follow our advice and wants the dog to have a litter of puppies.

Even worse – they then need you to assist with the birth and do a caesarean section! You don't agree with what they've done – but the animal needs help – how do you handle it and what do you do?

Euthanasia

One of the most common phrases that I encounter when I tell people what I do as my job, is 'Oh, I'd love to be a vet, but I wouldn't be able to cope with having to put animals to sleep.'

The correct term for putting an animal to sleep is 'euthanasia', which Wikipedia defines as 'the practice of intentionally ending life to relieve pain and suffering'. As vets, we are in a unique position to be able to end suffering of an animal, something which is not allowed, and is considered a highly controversial topic, in humans.

Putting an animal to sleep can be very sad, especially for the owner, but also sometimes for the vet. Dealing with death and having to be strong enough to provide support for people in that situation is a difficult part of our job and can be quite daunting at first. However, I have always thought that to be able to end suffering is ultimately a good thing, and being able to prevent a pet suffering and counsel people through what can be a very sad and stressful time can be a very positive thing.

Having end-of-life conversations with owners and putting animals to sleep can sometimes take its toll, but like dealing with any upsetting situation, talking it through with work colleagues or friends outside of work helps me feel better and focus on the positive outcomes and the good stuff. It is strange, but some of the times when people have expressed their gratitude the most, haven't been for administering life-saving medicine to their pet or doing a complex surgery – but for simply being kind and compassionate to them and their pet as it comes to the end of its life.

Grrrrr...

Further examples would be an owner who refuses to have their pet vaccinated, believing that vaccines do more harm than good (despite our scientific knowledge otherwise), or you may have to work with a farmer who has very poor welfare standards on their farm.

How do you think that you might deal with these types of situation, and can you think of other instances when simply trying to do your job may conflict with the beliefs of the owner?

Perhaps, most importantly though, being a vet can lead to so many different things. We will see later in the book the range of jobs that vets can do – and there are so many opportunities that I haven't been able to include them all!

I am a small animal vet – but while still doing a job I love, I have set up and run my own business, given talks to schools and other community youth groups about my job, written various articles for pet or vet magazines – and even written this book!

SO, YOU STILL WANT TO BE A VET AND THINK THAT YOU HAVE WHAT IT TAKES?

4. TO VET SCHOOL

WHERE TO STUDY

When I graduated from the Royal Veterinary College in 2004 there were seven places in the UK and Ireland where you could go to study vet medicine. The Royal Veterinary College in LONDON, and the universities of BRISTOL, CAMBRIDGE, LIVERPOOL, EDINBURGH, GLASGOW and DUBLIN, which all have vet schools. There are now two more places offering a degree in veterinary medicine - the University of NOTTINGHAM and the University of SURREY, and you will soon be able to study veterinary medicine at a new veterinary school that has been established as a joint venture between HARPER ADAMS and KEELE universities.

University, vet school or vet college – what's the difference?

There isn't a difference! We talk about vet school or veterinary college, and also university – but what we are referring to is one and the same thing. Vet schools or veterinary colleges are part of universities – which is why you will go through the university admissions process in order to get a place.

FOR SOME PEOPLE A PARTICULAR LOCATION MAY SUIT THEM BETTER, OR THEY MAY HAVE A VERY SPECIFIC REASON FOR ATTENDING A CERTAIN UNIVERSITY

– but most people are just glad to be offered a place at any of the veterinary schools, as ultimately, whichever one you go to, the end result is the same – you will be trained and qualify to work as a veterinary surgeon and eligible to become a Member of the Royal College of Veterinary Surgeons.

When this happens, you can use the letters MRCVS after your name, along with the degree qualifications that you obtained from whichever university you went to.

If you would like to know more about individual courses and the differences between them, additional information can be found at www.vetschoolscouncil.ac.uk in their guide 'Admissions processes and entry requirements for UK vet schools', and we will look closer at the entry requirements for veterinary school a bit later on.

WORLDWIDE LEARNING

BEING A VET OPENS UP OPPORTUNITIES TO WORKING AND LIVING IN NEARLY ANY COUNTRY YOU COULD HOPE TO TRAVEL TO. ANIMALS ARE PRETTY MUCH EVERYWHERE, SO VETS ARE NEEDED ALL OVER THE WORLD. SO FAR IN THIS BOOK, WE'VE LOOKED MAINLY AT VETERINARY EDUCATION IN THE UK, BUT THERE ARE HUNDREDS OF OTHER VETERINARY SCHOOLS **ALL OVER THE WORLD.**

Along with most of the UK veterinary schools, the University of California, Davis and Cornell University vet schools in the USA, and those at Utrecht in the Netherlands and Guelph in Canada, are considered to be among the best in the world, according to the QS World University Ranking (www.topuniversities.com). Numerous other good veterinary schools can be found across Europe, North and South America, Canada, Australia, New Zealand, Asia, Africa and elsewhere in the world.

What is very important though, is the quality of the veterinary degree offered at any institution, and where the qualification awarded will enable you to work.

In the UK, the Royal College of Veterinary Surgeons undertakes visits to vet schools to ensure that educational standards are met. In Europe, the European Association of Establishments for Veterinary Education (EAEVE) have a similar role for the European vet schools, and the American Veterinary Medical Association (AVMA) oversees the veterinary education system in the US. The AVMA states on its website that recognition by the organisation 'represents the highest standard of achievement for veterinary medical education' (www.avma.org).

I ASKED KATE COBB FOR ANY ADVICE ON APPLYING TO VETERINARY SCHOOLS OUTSIDE OF THE UK. HER ADVICE IS:

"Look carefully at the institution offering the course, and try and look in some detail at the course structure. Check which organisations recognise the degree course offered, and where you would or wouldn't be able to work afterwards."

Even degrees that are recognised by other exam boards often require some extra exams or study to enable you to work in another country – so make sure you have done you research before you pack your suitcase!

The other thing to bear in mind, is just because your veterinary degree is recognized and you can work as a veterinary surgeon, obtaining visas and other documentation to live and work in other countries can be very tricky. For study overseas, lots of thought and pre-planning is required.

Veterinary degrees approved by any of the above organisations are considered to be of the best standard worldwide, and some vet schools are approved or 'accredited' by more than one organization. For example, the vet schools at Bristol, Edinburgh, Glasgow and the Royal Veterinary College in London offer veterinary degrees that are recognised by the RCVS, and also by the AVMA. This means that with a veterinary degree from any of these universities, it would be possible to use your qualification from the UK to work as a vet in the USA and Canada (after passing the North American Veterinary Licensing Examination or NAVLE exam, the same as you would if you graduated from a vet school in the USA or Canada). If you graduated from a UK vet school that **ISN'T** AVMA accredited, to work in the USA or Canada, you would have to sit the Foreign Graduate Clinical Examination, which is a **MUCH** bigger deal.

Another example is St. George's University in Grenada, West Indies. It offers a degree in veterinary medicine that is recognized by both the RCVS and AVMA, which means that as long as certain criteria are fulfilled, veterinary graduates from St. George's have a qualification that enables them to practice in the UK, USA and Canada.

The AVMA not only approves veterinary degrees from vet schools in the USA and Canada, and the ones mentioned earlier in the UK, but also some of the vet schools in Australia, New Zealand, one in France, one in Korea, one in the Netherlands, and one in Mexico. Interestingly, graduates from AVMA accredited universities can also automatically work as veterinary surgeons in the UK, but as I mentioned earlier, graduates from AVMA-approved UK vet schools, still need to undertake a further exam to work in the USA and Canada – looks like we got a bit of a raw deal!

Since Brexit, when the UK left the EU, the RCVS has formed an arrangement with EAEVE, meaning that UK veterinary graduates can still work in Europe, and vets who graduate from the EAEVE-accredited European vet schools are able to register as a member of the Royal College of Veterinary Surgeons and work as a vet in the UK.

The RCVS has similar arrangements with Australia, New Zealand and South Africa, whereby graduates from the vet schools in these countries can automatically work as vets in the UK, and vets who qualify in the UK can work as vets in any of those countries, without needing further qualifications.

Add into this mix the European vet schools who offer veterinary degree courses in the English language, and that opens up even more opportunities for worldwide veterinary studies. Universities offering these degrees, such as Budapest, need to be EAEVE accredited if graduates want to be eligible to automatically work in the UK and Europe, but they offer an alternative solution to those wishing to study veterinary medicine in the English language, and who perhaps can't get into a vet school in the UK.

A LEVELS AND UNIVERSITY APPLICATIONS

In the UK, university applications are made through UCAS, usually prior to you sitting your A level exams, and so an offer of a place will be made to successful individuals that will be subject to them obtaining certain grades.

When you fill in your university application form, you will be asked which universities that you would like to apply to (see 'Where to study', or for more information go to www.vetschoolscouncil.ac.uk) and be required to give a personal statement. The personal statement is an important part of a veterinary school application, as you can list any relevant work experience, discuss hobbies and interests that you might have, and summarize the skills and attributes that you have that support your application.

We all know that getting into veterinary school requires you to work hard at school and get excellent exam results – that is a given. However, we also now know that there is more to being a good vet than simply being clever enough to get on the course, and so the applications procedure is changing, with greater importance placed on non-academic merits. In other words, just getting outstanding A level results isn't enough anymore, and for those who may not achieve such fantastic grades at A level (like me!), you still have a good chance of getting into vet school if you can demonstrate that you fulfil many of the other selection criteria. The other criteria being that you have, and can demonstrate, the necessary skills and qualities to be a successful undergraduate and vet, and that you have been committed enough to undertake sufficient, relevant work experience. We will look at each of these three areas in more detail later.

In addition to your UCAS form, individual vet schools or universities may request that you fill in their own questionnaire, and you may be invited for interview. At the interview, you may also be asked to do a simple test to assess your problem-solving or practical skills, or to complete a personality or a special kind of test called an 'aptitude test', which tests your ability to perform tasks and how you respond to situations. How you perform in the test is dependent on who you are as a person really, and it is certainly not something that you can revise for! There often is no 'pass' or 'fail' with these tests – it will just tell the interviewers a bit more about the sort of person you are.

WHICH A LEVELS (OR EQUIVALENT)?

Each university will have their own specific academic requirements, usually based on A level results, the International Baccalaureate or Scottish Highers. Graduate entry may also be considered at some universities. This means that applicants will have completed an undergraduate degree in a different subject already. Graduate entries usually require at least a 2:1 and a pass in one or more science A levels. Vocational qualifications such as BTECHs are occasionally considered, but it is dependent on the vet school.

The range of the academic qualifications required varies slightly between the individual vet schools or universities, so at the time of UCAS application you'll need to look more closely at the entry requirements to help you decide where to apply, especially if you are studying for Scottish Highers or an International Baccalaureate or have vocational qualifications. For those taking A levels, as a guide, the entry requirement ranges from two grade As and one grade B to one grade A* and two grade As. Most universities require a grade A in chemistry and biology and stipulate that the other A level subject is either physics or maths.

Some universities also have specific GSCE requirements. Again, you'll need to look more closely at the entry requirements for each vet school, but as a rough guide, most would require grades 9, 8 or 7 (or the points equivalent), especially for maths and the sciences.

Equivalent qualifications from other countries are also sometimes accepted – it is not uncommon for students from other countries to study at vet school in the UK.

To find out more about the specific requirements of each vet school you would need to check with the admissions team at each university, or you can find out more information on the UCAS website. The UCAS website (www.ucas.com) has loads of useful information about applying to university -- it is definitely worth a look.

If you don't have the necessary grades or qualifications in the correct subjects, some vet schools offer a preliminary year course, which brings you up to speed with the necessary maths and sciences before you go on to study to be a vet. This adds an additional year to your time spent at university, but is a great opportunity for those who really want to be a vet but don't fulfil the usual entry requirements.

PERSONAL SKILLS AND ATTRIBUTES

Lots of studies have been done to look at the attributes and personal skills of those that thrive at vet school and beyond, in a career in veterinary medicine – and the results have been quite interesting!

Although first-rate examination results are considered important, vets who had recently graduated considered brilliant veterinary knowledge to be less important to doing their job well than other skills and qualities such as integrity, friendliness, compassion and resilience.

In another study, a group of final year veterinary students and a group of vets were asked what they thought were the most important skills for their job. The vet students rated veterinary knowledge and being aware of veterinary legislation as more important than those who were actually working as vets. And those working as vets recognized that their communication and interpersonal skills were more essential for helping pets, managing owners and getting a positive outcome, rather than needing brilliant veterinary knowledge.

This is now widely recognized and is why universities will consider applicants that may not have the very high A level grades that have historically been required, but do show that they have the right skills and attitude.

Other personal attributes that were also rated as important for being a vet in the same study include:

- **THE ABILITY TO WORK UNDER PRESSURE**
- **RECOGNIZING YOUR OWN LIMITATIONS AND KNOWING WHEN TO SEEK ADVICE**
- **PRACTICAL SKILLS, LISTENING SKILLS AND THE ABILITY TO COMMUNICATE WITH COLLEAGUES, CLIENTS AND MEMBERS OF THE PUBLIC.**

Add this to the necessary skills and attributes required for obtaining good A level grades and completing several weeks of varied work experience and we can come up with quite a list!

HOW MANY BOXES DO YOU THINK YOU TICK?

- Friendly ☐
- Compassionate ☐
- Animal Lover ☐
- Caring ☐
- Integrity ☐
- Hard working ☐
- Motivated ☐
- Dedicated ☐
- Committed ☐
- Resilient ☐
- Understanding ☐
- Positive ☐

What other skills and qualities do you think that you have?

QUICK QUIZ!

I want to be a vet because…

A I absolutely love the thought of working with puppies and kittens all day, I'm horse-mad, and I live next door to a field of sheep so know exactly what it's like on a farm.

B I'm likely to get fantastic A level grades but don't know what to study at university. I've heard it's really competitive to get into vet school so it must be a great job – right?

C I love animals but also really enjoy working with and understanding people. I'm looking for a career where there is plenty of opportunity to do different things, and potentially can be very rewarding.

Congratulations! You've applied to university and have got into vet school! It's getting towards the end of your first term and your mates, who are studying for other subjects, and have only fifteen hours of lectures a week, are off to a music festival this weekend. You have an anatomy exam on Monday and need to revise. What do you do?

A Such good bands are playing! I never thought there'd be so much work and study involved. I actually might see if I can get transferred onto their course…

B Go anyway. I'll take a textbook and might read it. I'm not that fussed and will probably breeze the test anyway.

C Tell your mates to have a good time and treat yourself to a night out at a local venue if you can get some good revision time in today. It sucks not to be able to go, but it will be worth it.

Wow – time is flying by and you're now 'seeing practice'. You are at a busy small animal practice, two members of staff have called in sick and all the staff are really, really busy. A dog that has had an operation is in the kennel waiting to be collected by the owner and has done a HUGE poo. You spot this – what do you do?

A Scream and try not to be sick.

B Not much – hopefully someone else will notice soon – it really smells! You're meant to be working with the vet. The vet nurses or the kennel assistants are there to deal with this kind of thing.

C Tell someone – but offer to clean the mess up. You obviously need to check that it's OK to go in to the kennel and approach the dog, but as long as it is, you are more than capable of cleaning up the mess and changing the bedding – everyone else is busy enough.

Hurrah! You are now a vet! You are really looking forward to the next consultation as an owner is bringing Hugo in, a gorgeous puppy that they have recently picked up from the breeder. He's nine weeks old and so ready to have his first vaccinations. You are keen to get them started as there has been a recent outbreak of parvovirus (a really nasty virus that dogs can die from) in the area. You mention this to Hugo's owner in the consultation room and she tells you that she's been on the internet and read some bad stuff about vaccines – and decided she doesn't want Hugo vaccinated. What do you do?

A Oh well, it's up to her, you get to cuddle Hugo anyway – he's so fluffy and cute and you're running behind anyway, if you don't have to go through all the vaccine stuff you can catch up.

B You are outraged. You know best, you think Hugo's owner is an idiot and pretty much tell her to stop wasting your time and go elsewhere for Hugo's care. People can be so stupid.

C You ask Hugo's owner what specific concerns she has and listen as she explains to you that she doesn't understand why animals need vaccines every year when humans don't. She's confused and doesn't want Hugo injected with everything every year if he doesn't need to be. You acknowledge her concerns and tell her how we no longer vaccinate against everything every year, only those bits of the vaccine that we need to. You explain about the local outbreak of parvovirus and how 'at risk' Hugo is. You also have a chat about possible blood testing in future to see if Hugo has sufficient immunity or needs booster vaccinations – but explain briefly that this system isn't always fool-proof either. (Hugo's owner seems genuinely grateful for your time and says that actually, she will go ahead and have Hugo vaccinated.)

You are alone at the practice, one of the vets is on holiday so you are working the last two hours of the day on your own. You have a full evening of appointments, several reports to write up from a herd health visit and some phone calls to make (people are expecting you to call with laboratory results) – and in the middle of it all, the receptionist gets a phone call from an anxious farmer and tells you that he has a cow that's giving birth – but she seems to be in trouble – can you go out and visit? What do you do?

A Go into melt-down. You thought being a vet was about puppies and kittens? You didn't sign up for this!

B You weren't taught how to deal with this at vet school. You thought you were going to be administering cutting-edge medical treatment like Supervet! You tell the receptionist that you're overloaded and SHE needs to sort this stuff out! You didn't sign up for this!

C It's all a bit stressful – but luckily organization and remaining calm in a crisis are two of your top three skills! You prioritize. You tell the receptionist to call the farmer and tell him you'll be there in 45 minutes. You ask a veterinary nurse to get the kit you'll need ready and loaded into the car while you scan the appointment list. Luckily most seem to be booster vaccination appointments. You ask the receptionist (after she's phoned the farmer) to phone the customers that were due in this evening and explain what's happened, and re-book the appointments for tomorrow. The reports can definitely be written later in the week, and you briefly check the laboratory results – the vet nurses can pass the information on to the owners while you are at the farm, and explain to the owners that you are dealing with an emergency and will call to discuss them in further detail tomorrow. It's not a great situation to be in – but you'd seen this type of thing happen when you were seeing practice.

You went to the farm and ended up doing a Caesarean section on the farmer's prize cow and delivering a beautiful, fit and healthy calf. The farmer is so chuffed that the next day he turns up at the practice with a huge box of very expensive chocolates which he gives to you personally. You LOVE chocolate – what do you do?

A Tuck them in your bag and take them home. This is what you thought it would all be about. Puppies, kittens, performing miracles and being given chocolate …

B Tuck them in your bag and take them home. You really are a BRILLIANT surgeon. You deserve them.

C Thank the farmer and explain that you are going to share them with the team. It was a really stressful evening yesterday, and although it was you who delivered the calf, you couldn't possibly have done it without the other staff who re-organized and lightened your workload and got you ready so that you could attend the visit. You might be the vet – but teamwork makes the dream work.

Something's gone wrong. You accidentally injected an animal with the wrong medication. You asked the vet nurse to draw it up into the syringe, which he did, but you were busy and not really watching what he was doing, and you picked up the wrong syringe and then injected the animal. Luckily, it's all OK and no harm has been done – but you've made a mistake and it has scared you. How will you deal with it?

A Leave the profession. This sort of stuff shouldn't happen. I just wanted to cuddle puppies and kittens.

B You feel TERRIBLE. You NEVER make mistakes. This cannot be happening to you and you definitely must not mention it to anyone – they might think you're stupid. It was the vet nurse's fault anyway – he could see you were busy.

C You are a bit shaken. But you accept that sometimes things don't always go to plan. You have a chat about it with a colleague as you feel bad – but feel better when they tell you that a similar thing happened to them. You decide to take something positive from it – and look at ways to stop a similar thing happening in future. You are still a good vet. These things happen.

When I'm old I want to look back on my career and think …

A I got to cuddle SO many cute puppies and kittens!

B I made my millions and changed the world!

C I've been really lucky to have a job where I've been able to help people and animals. I've got loads of great stories to tell. It's been hard at times and I've worked hard. But I am grateful to have had a job that has presented me with so many great opportunities.

HOW DID YOU SCORE?

MOSTLY As You like the idea of being a vet and clearly love animals, but could do with finding out a bit more about the reality of life as a vet. Make sure you've done plenty of work experience, and try and get some at an actual veterinary practice. Being a vet may not be quite what you are expecting.

MOSTLY Bs You've got it all – the exam results, the work experience – but are you sure this is really the right job for you? Do you think you have the necessary communication skills, are you a team player, and with your perfectionist streak how do you think you will cope with sometimes having to compromise? Make sure you do some work experience in a veterinary practice but also some that involves working with people – to make sure that being a vet is really the thing for you.

MOSTLY Cs I think you've already done some work experience, and you have a pretty good idea of what being a vet is like. You have some good core skills that will help you along the way and it seems that you understand and enjoy working with people. You realize that being a vet isn't a perfect job – there is no such thing. You are prepared to work hard, but also not be too hard on yourself when things don't always go to plan.

Good luck with your university application!

WORK EXPERIENCE

One of the reasons to start thinking about what you need to do to go to vet school quite early on, is the amount of work experience required. If you want to be a vet it is expected that you can demonstrate a commitment to discovering more about animals – working with animals, getting close to animals to find out more about them, how they live, what they do, how they act, and their basic husbandry and welfare requirements. And what their role is – are they pets, companions, service animals – do they work or are they food producing?

There is quite a wide variation in the amount of work experience required by each of the universities, but all stipulate that there must be some evidence of time spent gaining work experience at a veterinary practice and in most cases the minimal amount of time required is two weeks.

IT MAKES SENSE TO GAIN SOME WORK EXPERIENCE AT A MINIMUM OF TWO DIFFERENT TYPES OF VETERINARY PRACTICE

It makes sense to gain some work experience at a minimum of two different types of veterinary practice – for example at a companion animal practice and a farm animal practice. It is also worth thinking about some of the more unusual ways of gaining work experience with animals.

Working as a vet you could be looking after a working police dog, a highly prized racehorse or a rare zoological specimen, or you could end up attending meetings and making changes to animal welfare legislation. If you get an interview at veterinary school, you want to be able to demonstrate that you have considered the wide variety of the role. Remember though, being a vet is also about working with people, so things like a paid Saturday

Vet school experience days

Some universities and organizations offer vet school experience days, or workshops and seminars aimed at enhancing your knowledge of the vet school application process, promising 'top tips' to help you secure a place. Some vet schools even offer a two-week summer camp! Although these types of activity can be beneficial – they can also be costly, and they are certainly not essential - and attending one is not going to massively enhance your chance of getting a place. There are loads of websites where you can obtain information about applying to vet school and there are other books like this one! Universities and vet schools also have open days which you can go to – which are free of charge – and likely to be just as beneficial.

job at a shop, or any voluntary work that involves working with people, is still considered relevant work experience, even though it may not be directly linked to animals.

Although work experience is important, your school work is more important, and all the universities stipulate that anything over six or seven weeks of work experience will not increase your chance of gaining a place. Some places require only one or two weeks of work experience, but state that it must be recent, usually within the last 12–18 months.

Probably the most important thing on any work experience placement is that you demonstrate you are observant, you ask questions and are interactive. This will mean that you get the best experience possible from your placement, and also that you are able to demonstrate at interview that you have applied yourself and learnt something. Universities aren't looking for people who know it all already, but for people who are interested, enthusiastic and able to fit in and adapt to new and different situations. Your work experience placements will help you demonstrate all of these things.

THE PERSONAL STATEMENT

Part of the process of filling in the application for university is writing and submitting a personal statement. This is an ideal opportunity to showcase your work experience, talk about your strengths, your personality and your interests, and highlight **WHY** you want to be a vet.

It's really useful to mention some things that relate to veterinary medicine that particularly interest you – for example, the use of antibiotics to treat diseases in animals, a welfare topic that you have come across, or an interesting case that you have encountered during work experience. However, be aware that what you mention on your personal statement you may be asked about at an interview, so do make sure you have researched a little and have plenty to say!

You might want to think about mentioning any part-time jobs you have had, or if you have done any volunteering. Although it may not be animal related, it shows that you have committed to working for a specific cause, which demonstrates many of the qualities that they will be looking for, and also that you have had some experience of what it is like to have a job and work. It also shows that you have had interaction with people in a professional setting – as we have already explored, being a vet is not just about working with animals, but also about being able to communicate and interact effectively with people.

You may want to include any hobbies or interests that you have. Again, this might be helpful in demonstrating skills such as commitment, teamwork, or leadership, depending on what you do. Remember that they are looking for people that will cope with the ups and downs of being a vet – a life outside work and hobbies are very important for this. Not all universities will call people for interview, so your personal statement is really important as it may be the only chance you get to tell people all about yourself, why you want to be a vet and to showcase your personal skills and work experience.

TOP TIP

Make sure you leave plenty of time to write your personal statement, you don't want to rush this at the last minute – and ask an adult, ideally a teacher at school – to read your personal statement and give you some helpful suggestions as to how it can be improved. Make sure you check it for spelling mistakes and incorrect grammar – first impressions count!

Straight from the horse's mouth...

I ASKED DR KATY COBB WHO IS ON THE SELECTION PANEL OF THE UNIVERSITY OF NOTTINGHAM VETERINARY SCHOOL, THE SORT OF THINGS THAT MAKE A PERSONAL STATEMENT STAND OUT TO HER.

'For personal statements, students need to demonstrate a broad understanding of the profession, not just traditional small animal practice or farm practice, and provide evidence that they have done some additional reading around the current challenges or topics affecting the profession.

When describing their own experiences and achievements we look for candidates who can link the transferable skills they have gained to the requirements of a veterinary professional. We also look for well-rounded individuals, so include everything not just activities related to veterinary science.

Although the personal statement is important, we are more interested in YOU rather than what you have written. Be sure that at interview you can discuss the things that you have written about in your personal statement. The vast majority of the personal statements are actually very similar, so it's in person that you can make an impression and really get the chance to shine.'

SO, YOU'VE GOT AN INTERVIEW!

Once the applications forms have been submitted and read, a selection committee, usually made up of university staff, will select successful candidates who they want to offer a place to, or some of the universities may compile a shortlist, and then ask people on the shortlist to come to interview.

The interview is likely to be held at the vet school and usually you are interviewed by more than one person – sometimes a panel of two or three people – which may be made up of people from the university, from vets who work in practice or other areas of veterinary work, and sometimes even recent graduates. Sometimes candidates are asked to fill in an aptitude test – this is a way of testing your ability to perform specific tasks and how you react to certain situations. It's not a test of knowledge – so there is nothing that you can really revise for – and luckily there is no wrong or right answer – it's just about you!

Some vet schools also ask you to undertake a practical task as part of the interview process. Again, they are not looking for you to know technical answers, they are just assessing how you deal with new situations or problems.

KATY COBB AT THE UNIVERSITY OF NOTTINGHAM DESCRIBES A TYPICAL TASK THEY SET, AND HOW THEY ARE HOPING CANDIDATES RESPOND

'Sometimes we ask candidates to look at an organ from the body of animal, for example, a kidney or heart – and to describe it and tell us about it. We are not expecting people to have an in-depth knowledge of anatomy or physiology, but successful candidates are the ones who pick it up, describe it, make some statements about it, guess what animal it came and what it does – and if they don't know – to ask us about it. At vet school we will teach them all about anatomy and physiology – but what we want is the task to demonstrate the students who are really interested, keen, want to learn and can use their own skills and knowledge base to get as far as they can.'

INTERVIEWS CAN BE QUITE DAUNTING SO IT IS REALLY IMPORTANT TO BE PREPARED.

Think about the image that you want to get across – someone who will be a vet in a five years time! Think about what to wear (including jewellery!), arrange to get there in plenty of time – think about important things that you would really like to say, and even about the way you will sit and place your hands during the interview, as positive body language is really important in the way that you come across to the interviewer.

A good thing to do is try to arrange a mock interview. This can be with a teacher, or even ask another adult that you know to do it – ideally someone you don't know too well – you want to practice how it feels to sit in front of and be asked questions by someone you are unfamiliar with. A mock interview will certainly help prepare you and give you some practice at talking to someone that you don't know well and answering questions that maybe you weren't quite prepared for. Ask for feedback and use it positively to improve your interview technique.

Tips for a successful interview!

Prepare! Arrange a mock interview and think about what you want to make sure you say about yourself and also how you would answer some of the likely questions that will be asked:

- Why do you want to be a Vet?
- Are there any particular areas of veterinary medicine that interest you?
- Can you tell us about any interesting cases?

Think about speaking slowly and clearly – take a breath and think about your answer before you respond to any questions – it's fine to give some thought to a question before you reply.

Sit up with your arms in your lap in front of you – not folded. Look confident, even if you don't feel it! And smile!

Make sure you are familiar with what you have written in your personal statement and can talk about the things that you have mentioned. If you have an interest in something or have mentioned a specific case – make sure you have plenty to say about it!

Do your research – look up the universities and vet schools online, or visit their open days. Know a bit about them – maybe about their areas of research, or even about the sports they offer and clubs. Usually you will be asked if you have anything that you want to ask them. It's always good to have a question – and it may be that you want to ask them further about something that you've found out.

Perhaps most importantly – remember that the interview panel are human and nothing to be scared of. Try to relax and enjoy the process as much as you can – you've got this far so they are interested in you – and the next step may well be the offer of a place!

I ASKED KATE SOME EXAMPLES OF THE TYPES OF QUESTIONS THAT MAY BE ASKED AT INTERVIEW. BELOW ARE SOME INTERESTING QUESTIONS THAT YOU MAY WANT TO CONSIDER SOME ANSWERS TO.

- Why do you want to be a vet?
- Can you think of a memorable case you've seen while doing work experience – can you describe it?
- What sort of roles are there for a qualified veterinary surgeon?

- Do you know of an animal science or veterinary related topic that has been in the media recently?
- What changes do you think there might be in veterinary practice and pet ownership in the future?
- What are your views on testing human medicines in animals?
- What do you know about the Dangerous Dogs Act?

- Someone asks you to dock a puppy's tail when you are a vet in practice – what would you do?
- What do you understand by the term brachycephalic, and what are the effects it can have on the animal?
- What are your views on annual vaccination?
- What do you know about using antibiotics responsibly?

WOW!

THAT'S A LOT OF THINGS WE'VE TALKED ABOUT FOR JUST GETTING INTO VET SCHOOL. IT MAY SEEM DAUNTING, BUT DO THE RIGHT THINGS BEFOREHAND, AND THERE IS A REALLY GOOD CHANCE THAT YOU'LL BE OFFERED A PLACE TO STUDY.

To learn more about applying to vet school, I thought it would be useful to talk to someone who's been through the process more recently, so I caught up with Henry, a student who has just finished his A levels, applied to vet school – and been offered a place!

Name: Henry Horne

Age: 17 (18 in 3 weeks if that makes a difference!)

School/career so far: Keyworth Primary School in Nottinghamshire and Loughborough Grammar School, Leicestershire.

Qualifications and subjects at A level: biology, chemistry and geography – I'm nervously awaiting the results which I get on the 15th of August!

So, you've just taken your A levels and have applied to vet school, what's happening with your application at the moment?

I applied to four universities last October – Nottingham, Liverpool, Bristol and Surrey – and was over the moon to receive offers from all four. I've chosen Nottingham as my firm choice with Surrey as my insurance offer.

I finished my A levels in late June and think everything went well but I'll know for sure in August!

Wow, you got four places! That's amazing! How did it feel to be offered a place, and what are you going to do this summer while you wait for your exam results?

I was absolutely thrilled when I received my first offer and to get three more after that was beyond belief, considering how competitive the courses are. I've got a couple of holidays to look forward to and I'm also working as much as I can throughout this summer to build up some funds so I can support myself at university.

So, what made you want to be a vet – is it always something that you wanted to do?

Growing up I've always had a strong interest in animals and the natural world and as I've gone through my school career it's developed into a passion for science and anatomy. Having a neighbour as a vet definitely sparked my interest and after being fortunate enough to do some work experience with her and other vets, it confirmed to me that this is what I really want to do.

"GROWING UP I'VE ALWAYS HAD A STRONG INTEREST IN ANIMALS AND THE NATURAL WORLD"

Did you grow up with lots of animals and are either of your parents or any family members vets?

I didn't grow up with lots of pets or surrounded by animals, the exception being Brian our giant African land snail, but my parents are both very passionate about nature, so a lot of my childhood was spent outside in the countryside or at farms and wildlife parks so I've also developed a love for the animal world. Despite my parents having a love for animals, neither of them decided to work with them, so I'm the only member of my family to follow such a career path.

Once you'd decided you wanted to be a vet, how did you find out more about the university application process and applying to study veterinary medicine at vet school?

Primarily, most of my information came from the internet and talking to my neighbour who is a vet. But as I got closer to applying, I learnt a lot about the course and the application process from attending university open days and talking to current vet students who I knew through friends and family.

What's studying for A levels like?

A levels are definitely a huge step up from GCSEs so despite doing well at GCSE level I still found the A level course challenging, especially at the start of sixth form. However, over the two years I was able to adapt to the additional workload and pressure and I found that consistent work outside of normal lessons really helped to set me in good stead for the exams this summer.

And what sort of work experience did you do to prepare yourself for applying to vet school?

I was lucky to gain a wide variety of work experience ranging from volunteering at a local horse sanctuary, working on a dairy farm and spending a week lambing at Easter. I spent a week doing work experience at a small animal practice and I was very fortunate to spend a week at a pharmaceutical testing lab in Nottingham, which was different, but really interesting.

How was the application process? What sort of things did you put on your personal statement?

Overall, I found the application process quite straightforward but my prior research definitely helped prepare me for it. Some of the online questionnaires were slightly unusual both in their format and style of questioning. The interviews were nowhere near as daunting as I thought they would be and I actually found myself enjoying all three of them! In my personal statement I spoke about my interest in the profession, what inspired me to apply, my academic achievements, a large section on my work experience (especially reflecting on what I learnt from it) and a bit about my extra-curricular activities and hobbies.

What were the interviews like?

As part of the application process I attended interviews for three of the vet schools I applied to and had to fill out an online questionnaire for the fourth. The format of the interviews varied slightly – with Liverpool and Surrey having a multiple mini interview format with several different interview stations, whereas Nottingham split their interview process up into a group activity, a practical section and a more traditional interview in front of a panel of vets, university staff and even a vet student. Generally, I quite enjoyed my interviews and found them to be a lot more relaxed and friendly than I originally thought they would be.

Do you have any advice for people wanting to apply to vet school in future?

I would say it's very important to research the courses and their entry requirements as early as possible so you can start gaining suitable work experience a long time before you need to start applying.

So, what are the three most important skills that you have that you think will be helpful to you in your career as a vet?

First, I feel that interpersonal and communication skills are vital to a veterinary career as although you are fundamentally working with animals, a large part of the work involves building a good relationship with other people whether they are pet owners, farmers or colleagues. Also, I believe that a strong work ethic is an important skill to have as not only is the course itself long and challenging, but also, as a vet you have to work long hours and may be on-call 24/7 so have to be so committed and dedicated to your work. Finally, I feel that compassion and empathy skills will be very helpful as a vet as you have to interact with people from all walks of life in a genuine and respectful manner to ensure the best quality of care for their animal.

And finally, Henry, can you complete the sentence for me. I want to be a vet because …

… I want to be a vet because it allows me to be involved in an area of work that I am passionate about, in which no two days are the same, and I will continually be challenged and be able to develop my skills as I move through my career.

Thank you so much for taking the time to answer my questions Henry – and good luck!

NEWSFLASH!!

Since this interview, Henry has received his A level results and did very well, achieving the grades required to take up his place at Nottingham Vet School where he is now a first year student!
Great news!

> **SO, WE'VE LOOKED AT THE PROCESS OF APPLYING TO VET SCHOOL, AND HAVE CONSIDERED WHAT YOU NEED TO DO TO MAXIMIZE YOUR CHANCES OF GETTING IN. FEELING EXCITED?**

THEN IT'S TIME TO COME UP WITH A PLAN. WHAT DO I NEED TO DO NOW?

8-12 YEARS OLD

If you are still thinking of becoming a vet, it helps to start thinking about it, even this early on, at school. Do you think you have the right personality and skill set? If so, you need to start demonstrating your commitment to working with animals and people, and also showing that you have given more thought to being a vet, than simply keeping a pet or riding horses.

Have you ever visited a pig farm or a chicken farm?

Have you ever looked at the labels on the meat, milk or eggs at the supermarket and thought about what the Red Tractor symbol on the packaging means?

Do you know why it is important to vaccinate cats, dogs and rabbits?

Can you demonstrate good communication and social skills, and have you had any work experience dealing with members of the public?

Trying to gain some work experience with animals is really important – and a great way to find out if being a vet is the right thing for you.

You might be able to help out on a local farm, or at a pet shop. Animals can look very cute in pictures – but working with them is not always as easy as it looks. You might find that there are certain types of animal that you really enjoy working alongside, or find that there are things about their care, welfare or management that really interest you – and finding out and being able to talk about these things will be really useful later on – for your personal statement, or if you get that all important interview.

12-16 YEARS OLD

This is a good time to start thinking about getting some work experience at an actual veterinary practice. It doesn't really matter what type of practice you go to, but seeing what vets actually do day to day is vital to ensure that you can imagine yourself doing the same thing in future.

Work experience at a vets can be quite difficult to get. Veterinary practices are usually busy places – but your school may be able to help you out. They may have had pupils go to a local veterinary practice before and can recommend somewhere, or it may be up to you to contact your local practices and see if they will take you. You only need a few days.

When you enquire somewhere about work experience, I always think that it is better that YOU make the telephone call or send the email, rather than your parents. Remember, it is YOU that wants to be a vet. Self-motivation, organization and having confidence when communicating with people are key skills to demonstrate – and what better way to show that you have these attributes by organizing your own work experience placement!

When you do go to a vets on work experience, do be aware that a lot of what you do will simply be observing and shadowing the vet or veterinary nurses. There is very little at this stage that you can help the vet with, though you might be given some jobs to do by the veterinary nurses! The main thing is that you get a feel for what vets do day-to-day, and what it is like to work in a veterinary practice as part of the practice team. Look carefully, and when you find a suitable moment, ask questions – you want to find out if this really is the right job for you!

IT DOESN'T REALLY MATTER WHAT TYPE OF PRACTICE THAT YOU GO TO, BUT SEEING WHAT VETS ACTUALLY DO DAY TO DAY IS VITAL

Do remember though, that working in a veterinary practice is only one option nowadays of being a vet – and there are so many interesting things that you can do with your veterinary qualification. We've looked a lot at getting into vet school.

NOW IT'S TIME TO LOOK BEYOND!

5. AND BEYOND

BECOMING A VET CAN LEAD TO **WIDE A WIDE RANGE OF OPPORTUNITIES** AND CAREER PATHS. THE NEXT SECTION OF THIS BOOK LOOKS AT THE DIFFERENT SECTORS THAT VETS CAN WORK IN, AND PROVIDES SOME DETAIL ABOUT THE VETS, HOW THEY GOT THERE, AND WHAT IT'S LIKE TO DO THEIR JOB.

IT'S BEEN REALLY INTERESTING TO FIND OUT ABOUT WHAT OTHER PEOPLE WHO WORK AS VETS DO. I LOVE MY JOB WORKING WITH PET ANIMALS, BUT IT HAS BEEN FASCINATING TO LEARN WHAT SOME OTHER PEOPLE THAT HAVE QUALIFIED AS VETS HAVE GONE ON TO DO. YOU CAN FIND OUT ALL ABOUT WHAT THEY DO TOO! BUT FIRST WE'LL START WITH **A BIT ABOUT ME.**

FACT FILE

BEING A SMALL ANIMAL VET

Name: Lorna Clark

Personal life: I live in East Leake, just outside Nottingham, with my husband and two children, two dogs, a cat, two gerbils, four tortoises, four giant African land snails, and a rescued Musk Turtle!

Hobbies: Cycling, baking, open water swimming and having a go at unusual crafts like glass fusion and basket weaving.

University: Royal Veterinary College, London

Year of graduation: 2004

Further qualifications: I have no further formal qualifications but received some management and leadership training in a previous role.

Role: Veterinary surgeon and owner/director of Pinfold Vets

Salary range: >£70,000

FACT FILE

MY STORY

I always wanted to be a vet – and this is part of the reason that I was so keen to write this book for you. I always wanted to work with animals and have told people that I wanted to be a vet for as long as I can remember. I did well in my GCSEs, but unfortunately, not so well in my A levels, and despite re-sitting them, I didn't get anyway near the required grades I hoped for, or needed, and so at my first attempt I failed to get into vet school. I was so disappointed, and felt really despondent.

Deciding that I needed something alternative to study, I signed up to a new degree course – Equine Studies at Coventry University, studying at Warwickshire College. I loved student life and excelled again academically as I was learning about something I enjoyed. All students were required to go on work placement for a year as part of the course and I completed my placement at the vet school of Edinburgh University, working for a professor of equine surgery, assisting him with research. It was here that I met lots of vet students and got an insider's view of the veterinary medicine course – and I realized that I still wanted to be a vet, and it was definitely the career for me.

I got a good result for my degree, and on that basis, on my second attempt at applying to vet school I was accepted at not just one, but three vet schools – I was over the moon! Despite my difficulties getting in first time around, I have never looked back. I went about my studies with enthusiasm, knowing that at the end I would be a vet. Seventeen years on, I am doing what I always wanted to do, I've opened my own veterinary practice, and still get so much enjoyment from the job that I do.

Getting into vet school isn't easy, but hopefully my story goes to show that A levels aren't the end of your journey. There can be other ways.

I am a small animal vet – and that means I look after pets and companion animals – mainly cats and dogs, but also other small pets like rabbits, rodents and guinea pigs, and I sometimes see more unusual pets like budgies, reptiles or tortoises.

My first job after finishing university was a mixed job – so I did mainly small animal work but did some visits to farm animals and horses – but quite quickly I found out that I liked dealing with pets and their owners at the practice. I also enjoyed doing surgery, and after a year or so, decided that I wouldn't do any further farm animal or horse work and instead, I would concentrate on expanding my knowledge and skills in small animal veterinary practice.

I have worked as a vet for 17 years, first, working in veterinary practices that were

FACT FILE

owned by other people and, for a number of years, working for a pet animal charity. Although this was hard work as the charity hospital was very busy, it gave me lots of valuable experience, and I then decided that I wanted to set up my own small animal practice – and that was when I opened Pinfold Vets.

TYPICAL DAY

Pinfold Vets is an independent small animal practice in a village called East Leake. I live in the village and my practice is just up the road from my house. What I love about owning my own practice is that I am in charge of the care that I give to patients and their owners. Working for myself means that I have additional responsibilities, and do not only the clinical work, treating the animals that get brought in to us, but also the management tasks such as employing and paying other staff to work with us – like veterinary nurses and receptionists, managing the accounts, organizing our workload, and making sure that our health and safety procedures and other work processes are up to date. Luckily, I have a business partner (who is also a vet) to share the responsibility and workload with – and we also have two other vets that work at the practice and provide care to our patients alongside us.

I quite enjoy the dual aspect of my role, and fit management tasks around the consultations, in-patient care and any surgery that I might have on that day. Setting up a practice is a big step, and you probably need a few years working as a vet employed by a practice before you do it – but it is very rewarding, and as the practice is successful, it means that I earn more than most other vets who don't work for themselves and are employed by a practice.

I start work just before 9am, after I have dropped my two children off at school. I then usually have some consultations and patients to see. Sometimes these may just be routine examinations – pets that have come in for their yearly check-up and vaccinations, or I might see a pet that has been ill or injured. Consultations in our

Vaccinations

A vaccine is a preparation (usually an injection) that helps provide protection against an infectious disease. It works by stimulating the immune system of the animal and in doing so ensures that it is protected against the disease in future. Vaccinating an animal helps keep it healthy and also helps control the spread of disease. A single vaccination does not last for the lifetime of an animal, and so regular booster vaccinations throughout the animal's life ensures that it remains protected from disease.

Vaccinations are widely used in veterinary medicine in all different types of animals – from pet rabbits to tigers in a zoo. Vaccine technology is so advanced, it is even possible to vaccinate chicks against certain types of infectious disease before they've even hatched out of their egg!

DO YOU KNOW WHAT DISEASES YOUR PET HAS BEEN VACCINATED FOR?

FACT FILE

practice last for 15 minutes, so it is important to work effectively and examine the pet thoroughly, and then discuss with the owner potential diagnostic tests and treatments.

Sometimes an animal may be admitted to the practice for further tests and treatment. If I do this, I ask the owner to sign a form to say that they understand what we are going to do with their pet, and also give them an idea of how much it will cost. This is when those people skills are important! We have to make sure that people fully understand what we are saying to them and sometimes we have to assist in helping them make a decision. Some people that come to see me can be quite worried and may be emotional during a consultation – my role is to reassure them, and help them out with their problem by doing what I can to help their pet.

At Pinfold Vets we have lots of equipment to help us make diagnoses and to treat animals. Some of our bigger and more expensive equipment includes an ultrasound scanner, a digital X-ray machine and processor, and a special table in our operating theatre. A lot of the operations we carry out are to neuter pets. We advise

"I LOVE SHARING PICTURES OF PEOPLE'S PETS, INTERESTING STORIES ABOUT THEM, AND TELLING PEOPLE ABOUT INTERESTING CASES".

that most people have their pets neutered. We do this because neutering has certain health benefits and can help prevent some quite common diseases, and hopefully we are also preventing unwanted litters of animals that then end up as strays or in rescue centres.

Sometimes we have to do other types of surgery – removing lumps or bumps, which we may send off to the laboratory to check that they aren't nasty tumours, and every so often we have to do operations to remove things from dogs' or cats' stomachs or intestines – things that they've eaten that they shouldn't have! I have removed pairs of tights, corn cobs, a baby's dummy, stones and a plastic toy, still in its case, that came from inside a well-known brand of chocolate egg!

These cases are really satisfying if they go well, as animals are really poorly when they eat things that get stuck – and once we've removed them, they feel so much better!

We try and get most of the operations and diagnostic tests and treatments done in the morning. Sometimes we end up doing more in the afternoon – especially if we have an emergency that comes in – for example, a pet with a wound that needs stitching up.

FACT FILE

In the afternoon we do some more consultations, or if it's quiet, I catch up on some work in the office, deal with my telephone messages and phone owners to update them about cases or give them test results. One of my favourite parts of the day is updating our social media page. I love sharing pictures of people's pets, interesting stories about them, and telling people about interesting cases. We get lots of 'likes' and some really nice comments and feedback too. These make me feel very positive about what we do.

Sometimes I finish early enough to collect my children from school, but as we are open until 7pm I have to do my fair share of evenings, so one or two days a week, I work until we close. When I work late, my children occasionally come with me to the practice (luckily, I am allowed to do this – as I am the boss!), but otherwise they go to after school club when I do an evening shift.

We also open on Saturday mornings and for a couple of hours on Sundays, and so we take it in turns to cover these shifts – I work about every third or fourth weekend and some bank holidays, but the good thing is, is that once we are closed, I can relax as the out-of-hours emergency vet takes over and I can enjoy my time off with my family.

BEST BITS OF MY JOB

There are so many positives to working in a small animal practice. I love meeting new people and finding out about them and their pets, and I really enjoy working with animals – and yes, it is true – as a vet you do get to cuddle lots of puppies and kittens, though there are lots of not-so-cute and unpleasant bits too! There will be plenty of success stories during a career as a vet to enjoy, and you will end up with some fantastic and very funny stories to tell.

AND THE WORST

A difficult part of my job can be putting an animal to sleep. Undoubtedly, this is one of the sadder situations that I find myself in – however, I feel privileged that I am able to stop an animal suffering, and do something positive for the owner, giving them support and guidance, and seeing them through those last few moments with their pet. You really form special bonds with people in this job – you can see folks through their happiest and most difficult times.

People's pets are often their best friend and I never underestimate how frightened and concerned they can be when they are worried that their pet is ill. Sometimes it can make people seem hostile or angry with you – but careful handling of the situation, listening to what they have to say, and lots of reassurance can often alleviate their concerns and diffuse a tense situation. On the plus side, when you

FACT FILE

help people and their pets, the vast majority are immensely grateful, and fixing a problem, being appreciated, or getting through a particularly busy and difficult day results in a great deal of job satisfaction.

Another benefit to working in small animal practice is the emergence of specialist 'out-of-hours' services in the last 15 years. This means that most small animal practices have a fully functional emergency hospital that will see any emergency cases overnight and even at certain times of the weekends and bank holidays. When I was first in practice, we used to take it in turns to take the practice phone with us when we closed – and would be 'on-call' overnight until we opened again the next day. Some nights were quiet, but others weren't, and I found it difficult to sleep when I had the work phone as I was anxious about being called – and if I had a busy night, I was very tired the next day. We also had no one on-call with us – so it was much harder and more stressful to deal with cases that required anything more than a straightforward consultation! Since that first job I have only worked at practices that use an out-of-hours service, and for me personally, I would find it difficult to go back to doing nights or weekends on-call, especially as I have young children. However, some friends of mine that are vets still have an out-of-hours rota at their practice which they take part in – but are rewarded well for it – either financially or with time off.

The harder parts of being a small animal vet are that the workload can be very variable – so sometimes you can feel quite stressed during a very busy day. Some people aren't always pleasant and easy to deal with and you may also have to make decisions based around what a customer can afford rather than what would be the best outcome for the pet, or maybe the customer doesn't share your views on what is best for their pet and so goes against your advice. Again, this is when those skills and personality traits that the vet schools are looking for are needed – resilience to help with those difficult to manage or less successful cases, patience and communication skills to help deal with an angry or dissatisfied customer, and a positive outlook and ability to work as part of a team – as this is what will get you through a challenging day.

I'VE REALLY ENJOYED TELLING YOU MY STORY. NOW HERE'S SOME MORE EXAMPLES OF WHAT OTHER PEOPLE WHO WORK AS VETS DO.

FACT FILE

BEING A CHARITY VET

Name: Joanne Trow

Personal life: I live in Nottingham, with my husband and two children, and Wilma the wire-haired Daschund!

Hobbies: Singing, dancing, eating, and visiting Scotland where I was born.

University: Glasgow

Year of graduation: 2002

Further qualifications: I don't need any further qualifications for my job, except some management training as I am a team leader.

Role: Veterinary Surgeon Team Leader at PDSA, Nottingham

Salary range: I work part time (19 hours a week). On a full-time basis my salary would be in the £25,000–40,000 range.

Joanna Trow

FACT FILE

MY STORY

After graduating I spent six years in a lovely mixed practice before I started working for PDSA at their Nottingham hospital. I had spent time at PDSA while I was at university and really liked the diverse range of cases and the ethos of the charity. PDSA helps people on low income by providing free or low-cost veterinary care for their pets. To me this is really important as I think everybody should be able to have a pet – you get so much benefit from their companionship – and helping people keep their pets and maintain that bond is amazing. I get real job satisfaction knowing that by caring for their pet I have made a real difference to a family or an owner.

BEST BITS OF MY JOB

The job satisfaction – and this can be from fixing a complex problem or just from providing advice and reassurance to a worried owner. Supporting people in times of need and providing a kind, listening ear means the world to people sometimes. Pets are such a positive thing in people's lives and the incredible bond we often witness between the pet and an owner is truly humbling.

> "PETS ARE SUCH A POSITIVE THING IN PEOPLE'S LIVES AND THE INCREDIBLE BOND WE OFTEN WITNESS BETWEEN THE PET AND AN OWNER IS TRULY HUMBLING."

AND THE WORST

Knowing how sad and lonely an owner will be at that point when a pet is suffering and it is time to say goodbye, though we always hope that offering kindness and support at this time goes some way to help.

MY FAVOURITE CASE

There are so many animals I could tell you about, but a really nice story is about Dolly, the Staffordshire Bull Terrier. Dolly went blind after developing a medical condition called diabetes. She was left with no sight whatsoever and her owner told me that she was often bumping into things, which she found confusing. Her owner felt upset for Dolly as she didn't seem to be enjoying life as she couldn't see where she was going – especially when she was out on walks.

FACT FILE

I decided to make Dolly a special collar, using extra-long plastic cable ties fitted to her normal collar. These would radiate out like huge whiskers and help Dolly feel her way around – a bit like her normal whiskers would do. Dolly soon got used to the collar and it really helped. Her owner was thrilled and so was Dolly. It helped Dolly get used to having no sight and she is now much more able to cope with being blind.

Dolly knows her way around her house now much better, but still wears the special collar when she is out and about. I'm thrilled to have helped Dolly – and despite all my specialist training at University – all I needed was her normal dog collar and a few cable ties!

TOP THREE ESSENTIAL SKILLS

Good listener, good communicator and time management – in this job it helps to be organized!

MY FAVOURITE THING ABOUT BEING A VET IS HAVING A JOB THAT STILL INTERESTS ME AFTER 17 YEARS AND MAKING A DIFFERENCE TO THE LIVES OF ANIMALS AND THE PEOPLE WHO LOVE THEM.

FACT FILE

BEING AN EMERGENCY VET

Name: Alyssa Comberbach

Personal life: I live in a little countryside village nestled between Nottingham and Derby, with my two cats, Topper and Clipper (both hand-reared kittens dumped at the clinic a number of years ago), my dog Frankie (the love of my life, also a rescue, found on a beach in Spain), a pony and my husband Phil. Soon to have an extra mouth to feed with a little baby joining us in the summer!

Hobbies: I enjoy spending sunny days outside with the pets, going on long walks, kayaking and riding the pony. I really am not a fan of winter as my outdoor life seems to stop for a few months!

University: Glasgow

Year of graduation: 2011

Further qualifications: I completed an internship and worked with some of the world's leading critical care vets – that was a great experience for me and I learnt so much. I am studying for a Certificate in Emergency Medicine, which hopefully will enable me to further my career prospects in this area. Extra qualifications are not essential to working as an emergency vet but generally further qualifications are required if you want to progress and become more specialist.

Role: Principal Veterinary Surgeon, Vets Now, Nottingham

Salary range: £40,000–70,000 (based on approximately ten shifts a month)

FACT FILE

MY STORY

I spent my childhood moving between countries and finished my high school career by doing the International Baccalaureate exams in Tokyo, China (these are similar to A levels, and thankfully recognized in the UK).

I knew I wanted to be a vet and so decided to come to the UK for university because of the world-renowned reputation of the vet schools here. Also, in the UK, you can go straight to vet school with just high school (higher education) qualifications. In other countries, getting into vet school requires you to complete another undergraduate degree first, meaning that your total education is lengthened by a number of years, and you accumulate more student debt.

I ended up going to Glasgow Vet School, a fantastic place, where I spent six years thoroughly enjoying myself and forming some incredible friendships. Halfway through vet school, I realized I didn't want to be a regular vet, and that I wanted to do something a bit more adrenaline-filled and exciting. I enjoyed surgery, and critically sick cases – so I decided that a career in emergency medicine was for me. I realized it wouldn't be easy to get straight into as a new graduate, but with the help of the university, I managed to focus as much of my studies as I could around emergency and critical care cases, and I volunteered with the emergency team at the university hospital. After graduation I managed to get an internship focusing

What does an out-of-hours service do?

Vets Now is an out-of-hours service that provides care for the pets of the local practices in the area when they are closed. This is quite commonplace now in small animal practice. We have a dedicated team in a fully equipped hospital that are ready to deal with any out-of-hours emergencies – which is far more preferable than dragging your own vet, half asleep, out of their bed in the middle of the night! We look after pets mainly at weekends, bank holidays and overnight, and deal with any new cases that may present and then our patients go back to their usual practices in the morning.

FACT FILE

mainly on emergency work. This gave me the foundations I needed to be able to base my whole career in the emergency and critical care sector which I love so very much.

I now work approximately ten nights a month, scattered between weekday nights, and weekends. We mostly see emergencies, which means you never know how busy your shift will be, or what exactly you will see! It is exciting, heartbreaking and incredibly rewarding all at once!

TYPICAL DAY:

Our shift starts at 6pm, when the daytime team at the hospital where we work hands over the in-patients they are leaving us. We then start to receive patients from other veterinary practices who need some care overnight. Most small animal veterinary practices nowadays don't have vets 'on-call' anymore overnight. They use clinics like ours to take calls and see patients at night. This means that the pets that come and see us at night get a veterinary team who are wide awake and ready to provide service and care as good as they would receive during the day. We are also open on weekends and bank holidays to do the same.

> **THERE IS NOTHING BETTER THAN REUNITING A PET THAT WE'VE HELPED MAKE BETTER WITH ITS LOVING OWNERS!**

Soon the phone calls start, when owners have returned home from work and found their pets unwell, or something has happened that evening that needs attention. We tend to be very busy with consultations until about 2am, then it settles down, we can get some dinner, and then type up our notes. If we are very lucky, we don't get many more calls through the night, so we can continue with any surgeries that need to be done, or patients that need diagnostic tests. Some nights, the phone calls don't stop and we see consultations all night, and try to fit in the in-patient care around the critical cases.

In the morning, we discharge all the patients, either home if they are fully recovered and well, or back to their daytime teams for continued care. At 10am I go home to get some sleep!

BEST BITS OF MY JOB

Dealing with very sick patients, where every minute counts – knowing that you are making a difference and potentially saving a life. There is nothing better than reuniting a pet that we've helped make better with its loving owners! I also love a good medical mystery, where you have to piece together the clues to try and figure

FACT FILE

out what on earth is going on, and then treat the patient!

AND THE WORST

Medical care for pets is not cheap, and owners sometimes think that because we work in this field, and obviously adore pets, that we should work for free. Unfortunately, a lot of owners have not got their pets insured, and struggle to pay for unexpected emergency vet bills. This often leads to angry owners, and sometimes animals left without treatment, which is heartbreaking and really does bring me down. We all want to be there for the patients when they need us, and to do our best, but sometimes the owners aren't able to afford the treatment that is needed. Speaking to owners who are angry with us about financial situations, often leads to a lot of stress for me and my team.

MY FAVOURITE CASE

There are so many great cases which I still continue to get a lot of joy from thinking about. But my all-time favourite, shows that animals and children never lie! Some owners brought in their very poorly Labrador with a very sore tummy. Having asked them if the dog had eaten anything odd, the owners reported that the dog would never have eaten anything abnormal, he was not a scavenger and never played with toys. The child kept tugging on her mum's sleeve and telling her that 'Mrs Lamb was at the tea party and George ate her.' Eventually, they agreed to let me take an X-ray of George, where, sure enough, there was a plastic toy shaped like a lamb in his stomach! Luckily, we managed to get Mrs Lamb out, and return her, almost as good as new, to her little owner!

TOP THREE ESSENTIAL SKILLS

Patience, ability to think outside of the box, and the ability to multitask!

MY FAVOURITE THING ABOUT BEING A VET IS ...

The satisfaction I get after a busy and difficult night shift, when all my patients get reunited with their owners!

FACT FILE

BEING A REFERRAL VET

Name: Anna Rix

Personal life: I live in Staffordshire, with my husband, daughter and two dogs – Millie and Mouse.

Hobbies: When I'm not at work I like to spend my time being as creative as possible with upholstery, upcycling furniture and painting. I also love listening to live music.

University: Edinburgh University

Year of graduation: 2007

Further qualifications: I have a BSAVA small animal ophthalmology certificate. This is essential for my current role.

Role: Small Animal Ophthalmologist at Pride Veterinary Centre, Derby – veterinary ophthalmology is a branch of veterinary medicine that deals with the diagnosis and treatment of eye disorders.

Salary range: £50,000–60,000 full time

FACT FILE

MY STORY

I always wanted to be a vet, but after some disappointing A level grades that wouldn't have been sufficient for me to get into vet school, I completed a degree in Animal Science at Leeds University. On the basis of my degree results I managed to get a place at Edinburgh Veterinary School, though I did a bit of travelling and worked for a few months before starting, in order to try to save some money.

After graduating I got a job in a mixed practice working with both large and small animals. I loved it, but decided I wanted to consolidate my knowledge of small animals and concentrate on surgery, so I moved into small animal practice and worked as an emergency night vet where I improved my surgical skills. I then moved into charity practice and although it wasn't something I'd thought of doing, I ended up as the senior vet, managing a veterinary hospital.

I had a short career break while I had my daughter and after returning to work, I decided to embark on a postgraduate certificate to study ophthalmology – a branch of medicine concerned with the study and treatment of disorders of the eye, as it's something I've always been interested in. After completing my certificate, I started work at a referral practice, working with other specialist vets, to treat referral ophthalmology cases.

Expert or specialist?

Vets that work at referral practices are usually experts in a certain area, or undertaking further training to become experts. Referral practices are staffed with vets who are considered leaders in their area of knowledge, and have undertaken advanced study and training and hold further qualifications. So how do you become a specialist?

After graduating as a vet, if you decide that you might like to specialize in a certain area you can apply for an internship. An internship is (usually) a 12-month placement at a specialist centre and is a stepping stone to a residency.

A residency is usually three years, and during this time you would work with experts in your chosen field to develop specialist level research skills and clinical experience. At the end of the residency you would then sit a specialist diploma exam – and at this point, if you pass, and can prove that you are a leader in your chosen field – you may then be awarded RCVS Specialist status, and then you can refer to yourself as a Specialist with a capital 'S' and have lots of other letters after your name.

Sound like a lot of hard work? It is! Luckily though, there are lots of other further qualifications that you can obtain while doing your day-to-day job in general practice which will ensure that people recognize your expertise, although you won't be considered an RCVS Specialist.

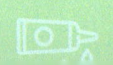

FACT FILE

TYPICAL DAY

As a referral vet, I see cases that are more difficult to diagnose and treat, and require more specialist knowledge for diagnosis and/or treatment. Most of the animals that come into the referral centre have been seen first by a vet in first opinion practice.

Working at a referral centre means that I work with other people that have further qualifications in my area of interest too. There is often quite specialist equipment – and we have some to perform surgery on eyes. This is quite different to other types of surgery as it requires very fine instruments and requires lots of magnification so we can see what we are doing. To magnify what we are looking at we use a special microscope or glasses called operating loupes.

My day doesn't really have a set routine – it very much depends on the cases that come in. If I have any patients in the hospital then I go and check on those and decide whether they need to stay, if they require any further treatment, or if they can go home. Whichever I decide, I usually phone their owners after I've examined them and give them an update.

WHEN YOU ARE ON-CALL YOU ARE REQUIRED TO DEAL WITH ALL THE EMERGENCY CASES THAT COME IN – AT ANY TIME, DAY OR NIGHT!

Routine appointments tend to be in the morning and planned surgeries in the afternoon. We will deal with emergencies in between. If there is no routine surgery booked in then I tend to spend my afternoon writing referral letters to the vets that have sent over the cases – updating them on the animal and any treatment.

I work one in four weeks on-call. When you are on-call you are required to deal with all the emergency cases that come in – at any time, day or night! – and even at weekends.

BEST BITS OF MY JOB

Making the animals better – especially the cases where the owner's think that their pet will lose its sight or even their eye! Getting to a diagnosis and fixing a problem is also very satisfying, and I love the relationships that build up with clients as you get to know them over time. It's also great to be able to support vets in general practice. As a referral vet, I don't just see cases at the referral hospital, but I often provide advice about cases that are seen by vets in general practice and discuss whether or

FACT FILE

not they need to be sent over. You might think that I would get bored dealing just with eye cases – but actually – I love it, and have really enjoyed doing further study to improve my knowledge in this area.

AND THE WORST

You can't always help every patient and some will lose their sight or even their eye, despite my best efforts. That never gets any easier to deal with. The workload can be quite stressful as we are small team and there can sometimes be multiple emergencies that come in all at once.

TOP THREE ESSENTIAL SKILLS

Patience, good communication skills and a sense of humour.

MY FAVOURITE THING ABOUT BEING A VET IS BEING ABLE TO MAKE A DIFFERENCE TO MY PATIENTS AND THEIR OWNERS.

FACT FILE

BEING AN EQUINE VET

Name: Jonathan Garratt

Personal life: I live in Quorn, Leicestershire with my wife and two daughters.

Hobbies: Cycling and triathlon. I follow Nottingham Forest (football), Leicester Tigers (rugby union) and the Dallas Cowboys (American football) teams and would prefer it if all were slightly better!

University: Royal Veterinary College, London

Year of graduation: 2004

Further qualifications: I completed the RCVS Certificate in Equine Practice in 2012 and am now an Advanced Veterinary Practitioner. Although this isn't essential to my role, it has improved my clinical skills and made me a better vet.

Role: Equine Veterinary Surgeon and Partner at Chine House Veterinary Hospital

Salary range: >£70,000

FACT FILE

MY STORY

I went straight to university after my A levels and studied veterinary medicine at the Royal Veterinary College in London. I loved horse-riding as a child so was always keen on working with horses, and after graduating I went straight into my role as an equine vet at Chine House and have been there ever since! I worked as a vet for a number of years before becoming a partner in the practice. Being a partner means that I part-own the business in conjunction with the other partners in the practice, and have managerial responsibilities in addition to my clinical role.

TYPICAL DAY

7.30am – I leave the house to get to stud calls. These visits involve using an ultrasound machine to scan mares and see if they are pregnant, or 'in foal' as we call it.

10am – I start morning visits to other yards, or head back to the hospital. At the hospital our time is usually spent investigating lame horses, treating the sick horses that we have staying with us, and anaesthetizing horses that require surgery.
This usually takes all day and is interspersed with phoning owners to update them on cases or advice calls. I usually grab lunch on the go and continue working on hospital cases throughout the afternoon.

6pm – I try and get finished and, providing all my paperwork is complete, then I head home. I am on-call one night a week and one weekend a month – that means that after 6pm I have to attend to any emergency cases that come in.

Out-of-hours work can be challenging. At first, I used to find dealing with the emergencies quite stressful, but now I'm more experienced, I find it's juggling night and weekends on-call with family life that is harder!

THE BEST BITS OF MY JOB

I do a lot of reproduction work and love it when I get to follow a mare from when she is first pregnant, to delivery of a healthy foal. I also like building relationships with clients – many have become friends and good relationships make my job more enjoyable.

AND THE WORST

Like most vets, I take it to heart if a case doesn't go well – and it can be made harder if the owner is upset and blames you for not getting the outcome that they wanted.

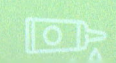

FACT FILE

This is always hard but does get slightly easier with experience.

PROUDEST MOMENT

Being made a partner at the Chine House Veterinary Practice. This was my goal after graduating and I feel proud to be an owner of such a large and successful practice.

TOP THREE ESSENTIAL SKILLS

Problem solving, good communication, compassion and empathy with people.

MY FAVOURITE THING ABOUT BEING A VET IS ...

The varied nature of the work I do. I have some days driving around Leicestershire doing very simple, routine tasks, such as vaccinations and chatting to clients on yards, and other days I see more interesting cases at the hospital that challenge me clinically. No two days are ever the same!

FACT FILE

BEING A FARM ANIMAL VET

Name: Rueben Newsome

Personal life: West Dorset, 15 minutes from the South Coast. The sea is a great way to cool down and freshen up after a summer's day working in overalls! I live with my girlfriend in an old cottage that requires continual care and attention.

Hobbies: Looking after and renovating our house, cycling, walking in the mountains and cross-country running alongside my girlfriend on her horse called Grigio – and sometimes I'm even faster than him!

Reuben Newsome

University: I went to the Veterinary School at the University of Nottingham. But it was a close-run thing. I was initially rejected from all the universities that I applied to – but was then offered two places on A level results day. It just goes to show the importance of not giving up!

Year of graduation: 2017

Further qualifications: I studied for a postgraduate diploma in Veterinary Clinical Practice (PGDipVCP) during my first year of work. This hasn't been essential to my role but provided useful clinical training with support and means ultimately, I can offer a better service to the customer.

Role: Farm Vet and Clinical Researcher for Synergy Farm Health Ltd

Salary range: £30,000–40,000

FACT FILE

MY STORY

I took a slightly unusual route through vet school, taking a 'break' between my third and fourth year to do a PhD researching lameness in dairy cattle. I then completed my final year of vet school, graduating in 2017. My PhD allowed me to develop other skills including project management, data analysis, scientific writing and presenting, and ultimately this led to Synergy creating a formal research role for me within the practice.

TYPICAL DAY

As a farm vet, some of my work involves diagnosing problems or diseases, treating sick animals (mainly sheep and cattle) and calving cows. Farm work, however, is rapidly changing and preventing disease and illness is as important as curing them. Prevention involves data analysis, herd health monitoring and consultancy, which is an exciting development for our profession and requires an ever-broadening skill set.

For the research part of my job I conduct research projects within the practice to keep expanding our knowledge for the benefit of our customers, patients and others in the profession. Examples of my research include developing new diagnostic tests, trialling new medications or vaccinations, or researching the efficiency of different farming systems.

My normal working hours are 8am–5.30pm, though sometimes I might start a bit earlier if we have pre-booked visits to farms. In the morning, I usually do herd health visits, pregnancy diagnosing and fertility work and surgeries such as castrations or removing horns, or disease investigation which may involve blood sampling.

In the afternoon, I often go tuberculosis (TB) testing and do health planning with farmers, or if it's quiet I'll go back to the practice to do paperwork, see my colleagues and drop off any diagnostic samples to the lab. I may get called to emergency situations like a calving which needs to be seen as soon as possible.

I will also be 'on-call' one night a week, or sometimes a whole weekend. Sometimes we get no calls, but other times it can be very busy and we get very little sleep. In return for doing the out-of-hours work I have a day off every other week.

Something I really enjoy aside from my normal work, is organizing and holding evening meetings about various topics where we teach our customers about something, or have a discussion about managing a certain aspect of health or disease. It's usually held at the pub – so it's quite a nice balance between work and social and offers a wider service to our customers.

FACT FILE

BEST BITS OF MY JOB

Bringing new life safely into the world is incredibly satisfying and I will never get tired of it. For me, this usually involves calving cows or lambing a sheep. Long term projects involving disease prevention or eradication are very rewarding, and working as part of a team with the farmer and farm workers when we are in this role makes me feel very positive about my job.

AND THE WORST

One of the most stressful parts of my job is when I'm in an unsafe situation. People working with large animals need to have good training in handling them and good, well-maintained facilities to restrain them in too, as these animals are strong and can be unpredictable and ultimately dangerous. As farm vets we need to keep physically fit and able as these animals can cause career-ending injuries, so safety on the farm for all concerned is extremely important.

TOP THREE ESSENTIAL SKILLS

Communication skills, problem solving, teamwork.

MY FAVOURITE THING ABOUT BEING A VET IS ...

Working outside with other caring and knowledgeable people, whether they are work colleagues or customers, to aid animal well-being and farm efficiency.

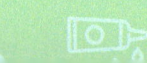

TB testing

TB or bovine tuberculosis (bTB), is an infectious disease of cattle that can spread from cows to humans. It can also affect other animals. In the UK, there is a comprehensive programme in place to try and eradicate TB, something that has been achieved in some other countries.

bTB eradication is one of the biggest challenges facing the UK cattle farming industry today. It is incredibly difficult to achieve, especially as bTB also affects wildlife, (in particular, badgers), which act as a reservoir for the disease and can transmit the disease to cattle.

The government stipulate that all herds must be regularly bTB tested – and how often depends on the area where they live. Vets are required to carry out a special skin test and based on the results of this test, they may or may not be described as 'OTF' or Officially Tuberculosis Free.

Finding a cow that may have bTB in the herd can have huge implications, not just for the cow, but also for the farmer. Part of the vets' role is to not only test for bTB, but also to advise the farmers on how to keep their cows bTB free and how best to manage an outbreak.

> **FACT FILE**

BEING A LOCUM VET

Name: Kate Adams

Personal life: I live in Christchurch, New Zealand with my husband Mark, our two-year-old daughter Saoirse and cat Ed. I relocated there 10 years ago after a working holiday turned into a permanent move. I love getting outdoors, running, biking, or skiing in the mountains. I also love having a creative hobby and am learning how to throw pottery. We are currently on a family gap year in the UK, I'm very lucky to be able to travel with my job and work flexibly – as and when, and where, I want.

University: I qualified in 2005 from the Royal Veterinary College, London. I went straight to vet school after A levels. I spent a year longer at vet school. In addition to the usual veterinary qualification, I completed an intercalated degree in veterinary conservation medicine in between second and third year.

Further qualifications: I regularly do continuous profession development, which is a requirement for all vets, but I don't have any postgraduate qualifications. Moving about and locuming has meant there have been less opportunities to study for further qualifications, but I don't feel I have missed out, as you can still be a good first opinion vet without having to take extra exams.

Role: Locum Veterinary Surgeon

Salary range: As a locum vet I charge a daily rate. This is usually between £300 and £500 in the UK but can be more if I'm working anti-social hours – such as weekends or overnight.

FACT FILE

MY STORY

I am a general practitioner with a strong interest in emergency medicine and critical care. I started out in mixed practice in Cornwall, then went to New Zealand where I worked initially as a locum, and then in permanent roles in mixed and small animal practices and an emergency clinic.

This year we've come to the UK to visit friends and relatives, and have decided to stay on for a bit longer, so I'm doing some work as a locum veterinary surgeon in various practices over here. The term 'locum' describes a member of staff who is employed on a temporary basis and fulfils the duty of another person while they are away – on holiday, or on maternity leave for example. It means that I don't have a permanent job but fulfil short term contracts – sometimes even just a single shift or a day, at practices or clinics where they need extra staff.

BEST BITS OF MY JOB

I love animals but what I didn't think about when I went to vet school was how rewarding it was to also help the owners. I generally love the people aspect of my job. I am also grateful for the variety of challenges my work brings, and the flexibility of having the opportunity to do locum work and combine a career with family, travel and a life outside work!

AND THE WORST

Being a locum vet means that I often don't work in one place for a long period of time so I miss being part of a familiar team. Getting used to the way different practices run can also be tricky and I have to be quite flexible and adaptable to meet the requirements of each individual workplace. Being self-employed I also don't have a contract that covers me for sick pay or holidays. So although I can take plenty of time off – I don't receive any paid holiday allowance which I would do as an employee.

Just like in any other vet job, the emotional toll can be hard, particularly when dealing with very sick animals, or challenging clients who might project their frustration onto you. It's a long learning curve not to take things personally and be professional yet caring. A wise mentor once said to me, 'no one cares how much you know until they know how much you care' – I think that's very true.

MY FAVOURITE THING ABOUT BEING A VET IS ...

Being able to combine a job I love with family life and travel.

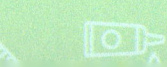

FACT FILE

BEING A POULTRY VET

Name: Emma King

Personal life: I live on the Isle of Anglesey and commute to, and work in, North Yorkshire. I live with my partner (a pilot), a Labrador, a Maine Coone kitten and two guinea pigs. I always wanted to be a vet and for as long as I can remember have been animal mad!

Hobbies: Climbing, hiking and eating!

University: I qualified from the Royal Veterinary College in 2016 in London, which I went straight to following my A levels.

Further qualifications: I undertook the Poultry Health Course which is run by Nottingham University. While not essential to my job, I found it very useful as it covered the subject in far more detail than we did at vet school where it is covered in only quite a basic way as it is a more unusual species to work with. I also have completed some Official Veterinarian (OV) training which has been essential for my job. OV vets do work on behalf of the government and we have to be specifically trained in certain areas such as exporting animals and disease surveillance.

Role: Poultry Veterinarian, Poultry Health Services

Salary range: £25,000–40,000 – working part time, three days a week

FACT FILE

MY STORY

Unusually, I went to university wanting to be a poultry vet. I have always had a fascination with birds and gained lots of work experience before vet school and during the early years at vet school. When I left university, I applied for an internship with Poultry Health Services (PHS) and am still with them three years later. PHS works with commercial poultry producers across a range of species including broiler (meat) chickens, laying hens, turkeys, gamebirds and the odd pigeon.

TYPICAL DAY

There is never really a typical day in my job. Poultry work differs slightly from the rest of the profession in that we manage our own workload, particularly booking routine visits, and do not have set times for consultations or post-mortem examinations. I usually head out to farms in the morning, sometimes for a routine health visit, or to investigate a problem, such as an increase in mortality (dead birds) or a decrease in egg production.

I am back in the practice most afternoons and will normally do two or three post-mortem examinations. In poultry practice we commonly carry out post-mortems pretty much daily – it is something that is done much less frequently in most other types of practice. A post-mortem is basically an examination of a dead body to determine the cause of death. By doing them, and taking samples to

Poultry welfare – in more detail

Strangely, one of the most difficult things I find with my job is the public perception of the industry that I work in. I frequently get asked how I can stand working 'in such a cruel industry' and that saddens me as the reality is very, very different.

The media are largely responsible, still using terms like 'factory farming' and implying that hens are still housed in battery cages (which is untrue – battery cages have been illegal in the UK since 2012!) Public opinion is often driven my media dramatization and based on very little knowledge or experience. To be told that barn eggs will no longer have a place in the UK market or that beak trimming will face a total ban is frustrating – particularly when the people driving such revolutions have never set foot on a poultry farm and have a poor understanding of the industry.

People forget that the poultry industry is actually made up of people, and the vast majority of the people that I come into contact with want to do what is best for their birds. I have seen laying hens with more toys to provide enrichment than the average child, and broiler sheds that are so technologically advanced they are like spaceships and regulate the environment so that conditions are always optimal for the birds.

I love the day-to-day clinical work of my job. Going to work on a site and looking at data, at the environment, at the live birds, at post mortem results and laboratory tests, and pilling it all together to solve a problem. I think it's a bit like a crime scene investigation – but with chickens!

I love the birds themselves; 10,000 day-old ducklings snoozing in a straw-strewn shed, 500 turkey stags gobbling enthusiastically at you, ten pens of pheasants sitting resplendent in the sun. But the area that brings me the most satisfaction is undoubtedly working hard with a farmer and seeing the results in terms of both bird health and production.

FACT FILE

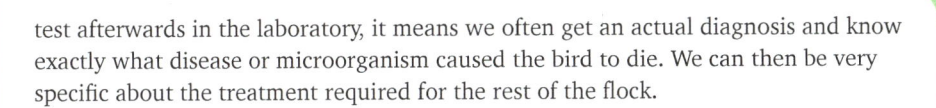

test afterwards in the laboratory, it means we often get an actual diagnosis and know exactly what disease or microorganism caused the bird to die. We can then be very specific about the treatment required for the rest of the flock.

Once I've done the post-mortems, I then catch up on phone calls and emails, check up on on-going cases, and then do paperwork – of which there is a lot in this industry. I also manage a large customer account so I will often have meetings and presentations to attend or will spend time analysing data I have collected to try and spot trends across the business to make it run more efficiently.

TOP THREE ESSENTIAL SKILLS

Resilience, organization and a positive mindset.

MY FAVOURITE THING ABOUT BEING A VET IS HELPING PEOPLE WORK WELL WITH ANIMALS AND SEEING THE BENEFITS TO BOTH AS A RESULT.

FACT FILE

BEING A ZOO VET

Name: Priya Bapodra

Personal life: I live in Powell, Ohio – about 10 minutes away from the zoo which is very useful for overnight emergencies and for my husband who also works at the zoo. We have cats which we hand-raised after finding them in a horse-barn when they were only 6 weeks old. Their names are Sparrow, Mo, Biggie and Hector.

Hobbies: Yoga, and challenging myself in escape rooms. I love travelling and photography and nature and often holiday where I can combine all three.

University: Royal Veterinary College, London

Year of graduation: 2006

Role: Senior Veterinarian at the Columbus Zoo and Aquarium, Ohio, USA. My primary role is to provide clinical care to the 10,000 animals housed at the zoo and aquarium.

FACT FILE

MY STORY:

In 2009, after two years spent working in small animal practice and completing a master's degree in Wild Animal Health, I was accepted into a Conservation Medicine residency programme at The Wilds in Ohio. At the end of the residency, I was fortunate enough to be kept on as staff at The Wilds, and then joined the team at Columbus Zoo shortly afterwards. I have been at the zoo ever since and I became a diplomate of the American College of Zoological Medicine in 2016 and an RCVS recognized specialist in zoological medicine in 2018.

Both of my further qualifications have been essential in obtaining my current role at the zoo. Alternative further qualification programmes now exist, such as internship programmes, and some sort of further qualification is pretty much essential for someone wishing to work in this field.

TYPICAL DAY

There is a vet at the zoo every single day of the year, including all bank holidays, so to ensure that weekends are covered we have staggered days off – I work Tuesday to Saturday. My working hours are from 8am–5pm but my days can be much longer, depending on what the workload of the day demands.

We start the day with a team meeting to discuss cases that need to be evaluated that day and the rest of the morning is usually spent with the veterinary team spreading out in different corners of the zoo performing re-check examinations or procedures. Some animals may come into the hospital for certain procedures, depending on the type of procedure and size of the animal.

> **I GENUINELY STILL GET GOOSE-BUMPS EVERY TIME I TALK TO SOMEONE ABOUT OUR MISSION AND SEE THAT THEY ARE GENUINELY INTERESTED IN WILDLIFE ISSUES.**

Afternoons are often spent writing up clinical notes, catching up on communication and planning procedures – which can take some time and attention to detail if planning an anaesthetic on a large, potentially dangerous or complicated species such as a gorilla, giraffe or rhino.

BEST BITS OF MY JOB

Knowing that I'm helping protect species sustainability and maintaining genetic diversity of animals under human care, which in the current climate of mass

FACT FILE

extinction of species, is really important to me.

I love being able to share our conservation message, our passion for what we do, and to inspire and educate people to care about wildlife and the plight of some animals in their native environments. I genuinely still get goose-bumps every time I talk to someone about our mission and see that they are genuinely interested in wildlife issues.

I so enjoy working with people who share the same intense passion as I do – the animal health staff, maintenance staff, zoo keepers – everyone definitely comes together in zoos to do what is needed for the animals.

AND THE WORST

The most stressful aspects of my job are also the parts I find sometimes most satisfying. For many of the species we work with we don't have a lot of background information, and some may be classed as critically endangered species. That brings a lot of responsibility, pressure and anxiety when trying to decide what is the right and appropriate treatment for an animal, while also taking into account that these animals are not domesticated and therefore can find treatments detrimental due to the stress of being handled.

The long working hours can also be stressful. Because of the specialist

The highlight of my career so far

One thing that I am immensely proud of is setting up the Giraffe Plasma Bank at the zoo, in partnership with Cheyenne Mountain Zoo in Colorado, USA. We have trained giraffe to voluntarily allow the collection of a litre of blood at a time using positive reinforcement, so that the plasma in the blood can be separated and used for any newly born giraffe calves in need in the USA. Sometimes if they are born very sick, plasma transfusions can be needed in the first few days of life. The plasma is a vital life support for these animals and they'd be unlikely to survive without it.

We currently have five giraffe at the zoo that are trained for large volume donation and have sent their plasma to nine different facilities to help their calves in need.

FACT FILE

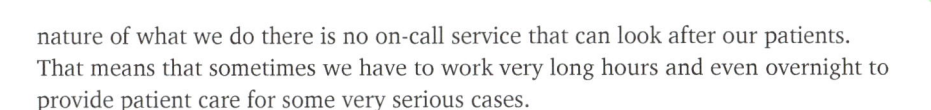

nature of what we do there is no on-call service that can look after our patients. That means that sometimes we have to work very long hours and even overnight to provide patient care for some very serious cases.

TOP THREE ESSENTIAL SKILLS

Good communications skills, the ability to assess and respond quickly to situations quickly and decisively, and creativity.

MY FAVOURITE THING ABOUT BEING A VET IS THE PRIVILEGE OF BEING ABLE TO CARE FOR ANIMALS AS WELL AS THE HUMANS THAT GO ALONG WITH THEM, AND AS A ZOO VET, CONTRIBUTING TO THE PRESERVATION OF SOME RARE AND ENDANGERED SPECIES.

FACT FILE

BEING A FISH VET

Name: Catherine Hadfield

Personal life: Although I'm British I spent most of my childhood in Malaysia and Europe. I went to university in England and then moved to the USA. I currently live in Seattle where I spend as much time as possible in the mountains or underwater.

University: Cambridge University

Year of graduation: 2004

Further qualifications: I passed the American College of Zoological Medicine Board exams which is the highest qualification in our sector of the profession – it involved lots of studying and more exams. I also passed the European College of Zoological Medicine Board exams. These qualifications are not essential to work in zoos or aquariums but they are increasingly becoming requested for jobs at large zoos, aquariums and those associated with universities.

Role: I am currently the Senior Veterinarian at Seattle Aquarium, Washington, USA.

Catherine Hadfield

FACT FILE

MY STORY

My story is a bit unusual and I took a bit of a different route to vet school. After my A levels I wasn't really sure what I wanted to do – I knew I enjoyed science, especially learning about aquatic ecosystems, so I did a degree in zoology. I spent two years doing fieldwork with humpback whales on their breeding grounds off the coast of Hawaii. That's where I realized that I liked the problem solving involved in aquatic animal medicine and I chose to go back to university to study veterinary medicine at Cambridge University.

During vet school I spent my summer holidays working for different aquariums and doing fieldwork projects. During that time, I carried out a research project for the National Aquarium in Baltimore, Maryland, USA, and the head vet there at the time encouraged me to apply for their internship when I graduated – and I got the position!

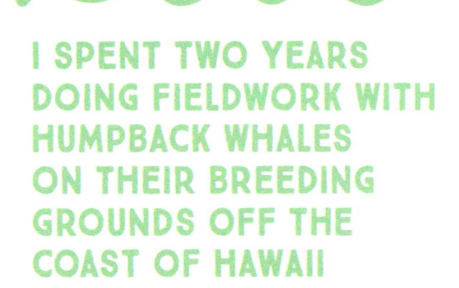

I SPENT TWO YEARS DOING FIELDWORK WITH HUMPBACK WHALES ON THEIR BREEDING GROUNDS OFF THE COAST OF HAWAII

That turned into a permanent job as their Associate Veterinarian. I had a really great mentor there who was instrumental in developing my clinical knowledge and professional skills. After 12 years at the National Aquarium I left to move to Seattle Aquarium and my current role.

TYPICAL DAY

My day varies a lot. Currently, it includes training husbandry behaviours (like getting voluntary blood samples from seals), doing routine examinations of animals, anaesthetizing fish and working on research projects.

I spend quite a lot of my day sat at a computer! I am the only vet at the Seattle Aquarium so I am always on-call, unless I can arrange for someone else to cover, but luckily emergencies that happen 'out of hours' are rare.

BEST BITS OF MY JOB

The constant problem solving involved in my job, the variety of interesting species I work with, and working alongside the wonderful and dedicated people who look after them.

FACT FILE

AND THE WORST

It is a very hard industry to break into. There are training positions and jobs available but there's lots of competition for them and they often require frequent relocation. The salaries are substantially lower than in private practice – especially for those starting out.

TOP THREE ESSENTIAL SKILLS

Good communication skills, an eagerness to learn and the ability to stay calm under stress.

MY FAVOURITE THING ABOUT BEING A VET IS THE OPPORTUNITIES THAT IT OPENS UP.

FACT FILE

BEING A RESEARCH VET

Name: Emma Drinkall

Personal life: I live in Nottinghamshire UK with my fiancé and my rescue Jack Russell called Mouse.

Hobbies: Outside of work I like spending my time taking on challenges and endurance events and travelling the world as we do them.

University: University of Nottingham

Year of graduation: 2012

Role: Postgraduate Researcher, Nottingham Veterinary School

Salary range: I am paid a stipend (like a salary, but less!) for doing my PhD. I also earn some money from teaching which I do part time, so it's less than £20,000.

A PhD is a research degree qualification that is awarded by universities, it is the highest academic degree that you can get. PhD stands for 'doctor of philosophy'. Study at this level usually involves undertaking a research project in a specific area, and those that achieve the qualification are recognized as experts in their chosen field. A PhD qualification is the next step after obtaining a master's degree.

FACT FILE

MY STORY

Although my PhD subject (Rainbow Trout health) seems quite unusual, it kind of makes sense to me as I grew up on a fishery in Cumbria. After graduation I also did a master's research degree looking at immune responses in cattle. During my research degree I learnt some really useful skills that have helped me with my PhD, and if I continue to pursue a career in research then a PhD is probably an essential qualification to have.

I have two roles in my job, which isn't that unusual for someone undertaking a research project based at a veterinary school. I am currently undertaking a PhD project, at the Nottingham Vet School investigating certain aspects of health in Rainbow Trout. This takes up a significant amount of my time spent at work, and the rest of it is spent working as a teaching associate at the vet school. This means that I help teach and deliver the Veterinary degree course to students.

TYPICAL DAY

My days are very variable, especially as I have two roles. Some days I might be working on my PhD – so in the laboratory trying to demonstrate a novel gene sequence in the DNA of my trout – and other days I might be teaching students how to take a biopsy sample, interpret a microscope slide or take a radiograph. I love the variety!

BEST BITS OF MY JOB

As a researcher I love coming up with ideas and working to solve them – it's all a puzzle. It's really satisfying when I get results and find out something new.

AND THE WORST

The amount of paperwork and all the rules and regulations that have to be followed when working in research can be quite daunting and it's frustrating that it means nothing can ever happen particularly quickly. It tests my patience sometimes but I just have to think that it will happen eventually.

TOP THREE ESSENTIAL SKILLS

Communication, passion, strong work ethic.

MY FAVOURITE THING ABOUT BEING A VET IS ...

The people and animals that I meet along the way in so many different roles – I will NEVER get bored!

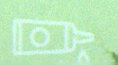

FACT FILE

BEING A VET IN EDUCATION

Name: Kate Cobb

Lives: I live in Sutton Bonington, close to Nottingham (and the vet school), with my husband Malcolm and two children Steph and Jack. I have a dog called Sylvester and I enjoy walking with him and friends from the village.

Hobbies: When I'm not at work I enjoy socializing with friends and family, keeping fit and walking the dog.

University: Royal Veterinary College, London

Year of graduation: 1996

Role: I am currently responsible for education and the student experience at Nottingham Veterinary School. This mainly involves making sure that we are teaching the right things at the highest standard to our vet students, ensuring that they get the best possible teaching experience. I also oversee the postgraduate processes too – the master's degrees and PhD projects.

Salary range: £40,000–70,000

FACT FILE

MY STORY

I went to university straight from school and started a family soon after graduating. After a number of years in veterinary practice, I decided to go into teaching as it fitted around family life. I have a PGCE in secondary science from the Brunel University and taught science to 11–19-year olds for two years.

Later on, I completed a master's degree in Medical Education at Nottingham University and I also have a PhD in Veterinary Education. My PhD research was on assessment of veterinary students and how this prepares them for starting clinical practice once they qualify. Because of my further work I am also a Senior Fellow of the Higher Education Academy – a governing body that oversees further qualifications. My further qualifications have been necessary for me to progress to my current role in education, although it is possible to enter veterinary education and academia without them and complete the relevant further qualifications as you go.

TYPICAL DAY

I don't really have a typical day as my days are really varied. Sometimes I'm teaching vet students at the university or in practice, or I may be attending various meetings. The variety of my role is something that I really enjoy.

BEST BITS OF MY JOB

Seeing vet students' progress through the course and going onto work and enjoy being part of the veterinary profession – it's great to think that I helped make that happen.

AND THE WORST

One of the most difficult parts of my role is managing people. We have over 100 teaching staff and 700 students – and it is impossible to please them all!

TOP THREE ESSENTIAL SKILLS

Communication skills, organization and flexibility.

MY FAVOURITE THING ABOUT BEING A VET IS …

The opportunities that it has brought me. Veterinary education is something that I never thought I would be involved with but it is a really rewarding job.

FACT FILE

BEING A VET IN INDUSTRY

Name: Michael Unsworth

Personal life: I live on the south coast near the South Downs with my husband, my two dogs – Rhubarb and Pudding and my three cats – Bam Bam, Gnocchi and Rocket. I like to spend my time walking the dogs, exercising at the gym or cooking something tasty!

University: Royal Veterinary College, London

Year of graduation: 2004

Further qualifications: None are necessary for my current job – but I have had to learn a lot more about pet nutrition.

Role: Associate Veterinary Affairs Manager

Salary range: >£70,000

Michael Unsworth

FACT FILE

MY STORY

I went to vet school straight after finishing my A levels. I couldn't wait to get started – I had always wanted to be a vet. While I was at school, I had a weekend job working in a shop. I think this really helped me to learn to deal with people as customers – especially my own customers when I finally qualified and was working as a vet.

I spent 11 years as a vet in practice. I particularly enjoyed the part of my job where I taught people how things worked and how we could fix them. That's why I chose to leave practice and work as a vet in industry – I no longer see animals and their owners, but I educate vets and nurses about the special food that the company I work for makes – which can help make sick pets better.

TYPICAL DAY

It's probably easier to describe a typical week as my days are often very different. I typically spend about two days in the office, working with other parts of the business, providing advice, training teams and responding to enquiries.

The other three days will generally be a mix of spending time working with our sales team and visiting veterinary practices with them. We also go and see specialist veterinary practices to discuss our products and provide information and teach about nutrition to vet students at the different veterinary schools. Sometimes I also get to work from home for the odd day.

BEST BITS OF MY JOB

Knowing that I'm helping to improve the health of pets by educating vets and nurses on nutrition. Hopefully that results in pets living healthier, longer and happier lives.

AND THE WORST

I spend a lot of time travelling for my job – so lots of driving and sometimes staying away from home. This can be really tiring and I don't like being away from home – so for me, this is probably the hardest part of my job.

TOP THREE ESSENTIAL SKILLS

Communications skills – I spend a lot of time talking to groups of people. I not only have to explain things clearly so that they understand them, but also make what I'm saying sound fun and interesting.

FACT FILE

People skills – Doing my job, first impressions are really important. I need people to feel comfortable around me and happy to ask questions or approach me for help if they need it.

Passion and belief – I could only be able to work in this type of job if I can genuinely be proud of the company that I work for and the products that we sell. The company I work for has improving animal health at the heart of everything it does – and people can tell that I'm passionate about what I do – which makes them much more likely to listen and think about what we're discussing.

MY FAVOURITE THING ABOUT BEING A VET IS

Being in the incredibly privileged position to work to help animals and their owners – often at difficult and stressful times. Being a vet opens so may doors: to be able to work anywhere in the world and really do any job you like.

UPDATE

Michael has recently moved to Spain to take up a job working as a Senior Veterinary Affairs Manager, across Europe, for another veterinary nutrition company. It really goes to prove that you never know where your job as a vet could take you!

FACT FILE

BEING A VET IN AFRICA

Name: James Kithuka

Occupation/role: Veterinary surgeon/animal welfare officer for the Brooke animal charity (www.thebrooke.org)

Qualifications and University attended: Bachelor of Veterinary Medicine (University of Nairobi, Kenya) and Master of Science in Veterinary Public Health (University of Nairobi, Kenya)

Year of qualification: BVM (1999); MSc VPH (2002)

James Kithuka

FACT FILE

DOES YOUR VETERINARY QUALIFICATION ALLOW YOU TO WORK IN OTHER STATES/COUNTRIES?

My qualification allows me to work in many states in Africa, but every state has their own regulations that have to be met before actually starting to work. This can be things like undergoing either a test, or maybe registration with their respective state animal health regulatory bodies.

MY STORY

I live in Kenya and work for Brooke, an international charity that protects and improves the lives of horses, donkeys and mules in the developing world. I basically train partner vets on various aspects of animal welfare, especially equine welfare – things like handling, physical examination, clinical reasoning, and treatment. I also train horse and donkey owners on various aspects of animal welfare issues especially those that can positively impact the lives of the animals and help prevent disease. We provide training to improve the care of horses and donkeys, looking at appropriate harnessing, proper feeding, disease prevention and management of minor ailments.

As well as my work with animals, I work with government officials in formulating and implementing equine welfare friendly policies and by-laws to help protect working animals. I also assist our partner projects in coming up with programmes that are equine welfare friendly and supporting them to implement those programmes based on our charity's guidelines, vision and mission.

THREE THINGS YOU ENJOY ABOUT BEING A VET:

1. Treating animals makes me happy because you directly help an animal that is in pain and cannot speak. After treatment they respond and one can see them happy and enjoying their lives once more.
2. Interacting with farmers and helping their animals makes me happy as feedback received indicates that I help their livelihoods too in addition to the life of animals.
3. I too like teaching/mentoring and transferring some practical veterinary competencies to my junior veterinarians and all animal health practitioners. This makes me feel rejoiced, happy and helps me not only give back to the society but makes me realize that through this I ultimately reach more animals in the world.

FACT FILE

BEING A GOVERNMENT VETERINARY OFFICER

Name: Amy Beckett

Personal life: I live on the Isle of Man with my dog Lola.

Hobbies: Walking on the beach, clay pigeon shooting and cycling.

University: Royal Veterinary College, London

Year of graduation: 2004

Further qualifications: Although my further qualifications (see My Story below) aren't essential for the role as a government vet, they were useful for my application as they demonstrated my knowledge of public health and disease control.

Role: Government Veterinary Officer

Salary range: £40,000–70,000 full time

FACT FILE

MY STORY

I went to secondary school and then did my A levels. I went straight to vet school after my A levels and then worked in veterinary practice for nine years. I decided to gain some further qualifications and so completed a master's degree in One Health (the cross-over between human and animal health) and a PhD in Immunology at Edinburgh University.

After completing my studies, I really wanted a position that required both my clinical veterinary experience and also my postgraduate qualifications. I saw the job for the Government Veterinary Officer on the Isle of Man advertised, so I applied – and got it!

TYPICAL DAY

I am involved with disease control, import and export of animals to and from the Isle of Man, animal welfare and disease outbreaks on the island, and various aspects of government policy and regulations. My days are very variable. I inspect riding schools, kennels, catteries and the wildlife park on the island and I may also have to visit welfare cases. For example – someone may have reported seeing some farm animals that they think aren't being well looked after. I also inspect and test animals that are imported to the Isle of Man for diseases, and I have to make sure that they come here following the correct procedures and with the correct paperwork. Animals travelling between countries pose a very significant risk of introducing disease – one of the reasons why my role as the government vet is important.

As well as being out on visits I also spend time in the office. I give advice to government ministers and to practising vets on the island. I also spend time contingency planning for a sudden disease outbreak, just in case!

I work mainly office hours so 9am to 5pm during the week, and don't do any official out-of-hours duties, but I could be contacted in an emergency, should there be a notifiable disease outbreak or something similar – but luckily situations like that are quite rare.

BEST BITS OF MY JOB

Knowing that I help safeguard the welfare of animals on the island and keep it free of certain diseases. This is particularly important for the farming industry and livestock on the island. I also work more regular hours than vets working in practice. Occasionally I have to work in the evening and rarely at a weekend – but certainly a lot less than I would as a traditional vet in practice.

FACT FILE

AND THE WORST

For me, the welfare visits are probably the most stressful and difficult to deal with – sometimes I have to deal with situations where animals aren't being very well looked after, and this can be frustrating and upsetting. There is also lots of quite restrictive legislation on the Isle of Man – and it can be difficult ensuring that people are compliant.

TOP THREE ESSENTIAL SKILLS

The ability to remain calm in a stressful situation, good communication skills – as I'm often required to deal with members of the public, and leadership – for when I'm required to manage other members of the team.

MY FAVOURITE THING ABOUT BEING A VET IS …

The freedom and ability it gives me to do a variety of interesting jobs.

Notifiable disease – foot and mouth

A notifiable disease is a disease that, by law, you have to report to the Animal and Plant Health Agency (APHA), an agency which works for the government Department for Environment Food and Rural Affairs (Defra) in the UK.

A disease becomes notifiable because of its importance, maybe in terms of commercial cost or risk to public health. Some notifiable diseases will be exotic, that is, not usually present in the UK, and so we want to manage any disease outbreak early so that we remain free of the disease. An example of an exotic notifiable disease is foot and mouth disease of which there was an outbreak in the UK in 2001, which had a significant negative impact on farming and tourism until it was controlled and eradicated. Previous to this, foot and mouth disease hadn't been present in the UK since 1967.

Other notifiable diseases are classed as endemic, which means they are present in the UK, but new cases have to be reported so that the disease can be carefully monitored and controlled. Bovine TB is an endemic notifiable disease. You can learn more about bovine TB with our farm vet.

6. MEMORABLE AND INTERESTING CASES

We've looked at lots of different types of vets. Some no longer work directly with animals, but are proud to remain members of the veterinary profession and fulfil other vital roles.

The vast majority of people who got to vet school do so because they want to do a job where they look after animals, diagnose disease and make animals better, and despite all the different roles that we've talked about, the majority of people who qualify as a vet and join the RCVS will end up doing just that.

> SO, THAT GOT ME THINKING ABOUT WHAT ELSE WOULD PEOPLE LIKE TO READ ABOUT IN MY BOOK. WE'VE TALKED LOTS ABOUT GOING TO VET SCHOOL, WE'VE TALKED ABOUT THE SKILLS YOU NEED AND THE QUALIFICATIONS. WE'VE LOOKED AT WHAT BEING A VET IS REALLY LIKE. BUT THE BOOK WOULDN'T BE COMPLETE WITHOUT ME WRITING ABOUT SOME OF MY MOST MEMORABLE AND INTERESTING CASES AND SHOWING YOU A FEW PICTURES ...

C

Conan the calf

ALTHOUGH FOR THE MAJORITY OF MY CAREER I'VE BEEN A SMALL ANIMAL VET, THE FIRST JOB I HAD AFTER I QUALIFIED WAS IN A MIXED PRACTICE AND OCCASIONALLY, I WOULD END UP HAVING TO GO OUT ON A VISIT TO SEE A SHEEP OR A COW.

One weekend I got called out by a farmer as he had a rare-breed cow that was struggling to give birth. Sometimes the calves aren't in the right position inside the cow, or there can be other problems which prevent a normal birth – and the calf can get stuck, and then both the cow and the calf are in danger. When this happens – the farmer calls the vet!

It was the first time I had ever been to calve a cow on my own, and although I was trying to look confident, inside I was feeling nervous. When I arrived, the farmer took me to the cow, I put on my long plastic gloves, and felt inside the cow. The calf was big, so big I think that the cow had probably run out of energy trying to push it out, but to my relief, I could feel the calf's nose and his front feet either side – so I knew he was in the right position to come out, and thought that we could probably get him out the natural way with some assistance, rather than having to do an operation (a Caesarean section).

Carefully I put ropes around the front feet of the calf and asked the farmer's sons (who had come out to see what was going on) to help hold them in position. While moving my hand over the back of the calf's head I asked my helpers to pull gently on the feet ropes, and we gradually eased the calf out from inside the cow, out into the big wide world. After a few minutes of gentle pulling (and after a big grunt from the cow), the calf plopped all the way out and onto the thick straw that was covering the floor. The calf sat up, shook his head and the cow turned around and licked him – it was lovely to see. Soon the calf was standing up – a bit wobbly on his legs – but he was a beautiful fit and healthy calf and the farmer was thrilled.

SOON THE CALF WAS STANDING UP – A BIT WOBBLY ON HIS LEGS – BUT HE WAS A BEAUTIFUL FIT AND HEALTHY CALF AND THE FARMER WAS THRILLED

Feeling good, I went home. A few weeks later an envelope arrived for me at work. Inside was a note from the farmer thanking me for looking after his cow and delivering her calf safely – and a photograph of the calf who was now called 'Conan' enjoying the sunshine out in the field.

I still have that photograph. It's a great reminder of some of the high points of my first year as a vet. There's still something really special about bringing new life into the world – no matter what type of animal it is!

Tizer – The dog who ran out of fizz

IT WAS A WEEKEND (AGAIN!) AND TIZER THE DOG WAS BROUGHT IN BY SOMEONE THAT WAS LOOKING AFTER HIM, AS HIS OWNERS WERE ON HOLIDAY. THEY WERE DISTRAUGHT AS TIZER WAS FINE THE DAY BEFORE, BUT TODAY, WAS COMPLETELY UNABLE TO WALK OR EVEN STAND.

He had to be carried into the vets, and he just lay on the floor looking up at me. It was a bit strange though, as usually when this sort of thing happens to dogs, they are so poorly and exhausted, they look really sad and have almost given up – but it was different with Tizer, he was lolling about on the floor, but very pleased to see me and still wagging his tail!

I examined Tizer and spoke to his owners who were away, and very worried – they were concerned that Tizer was so ill that he might die or have to be put to sleep. It was a Sunday, so there was no other vet working with me to talk about the case with, so I decided that there was something possibly quite unusual going on, and as I didn't know what – I put Tizer on a drip so he wouldn't get dehydrated, and decided that we would keep him at the vets overnight and examine him again the next day.

The next morning Tizer looked a bit better initially and was trying to stand up, but as the day passed, he got weaker and weaker again. We were unable to refer Tizer to a specialist and, confused by the unusual presentation, I was no further to reaching a diagnosis and was running out of options.

A SPECIALIST NEUROLOGIST FROM THE VETERINARY SCHOOL AT THE UNIVERSITY OF NOTTINGHAM AGREED THAT, AS IT WAS QUITE A STRANGE CASE, HE WOULD COME AND EXAMINE TIZER

Luckily in our profession there are always people to help, and a specialist neurologist from the Veterinary School at the University of Nottingham agreed that, as it was quite a strange case, he would come and examine Tizer for me.

After a thorough examination, he concluded that Tizer had a condition called myaesthenia gravis, a very rare disease of the neurological system, where Tizer's own immune cells attack his neurotransmitters. Put simply, this means that Tizer's nervous system runs out of charge or as I like to put it – Tizer had gone flat, and run out of fizz. What could we do? Luckily there was a drug that we could use to treat the condition. We would have to give some to Tizer and keep our fingers crossed that it would work.

We got some of the special medication for Tizer and gave it to him. The transformation was remarkable. The following day, Tizer could stand up. The day after, Tizer could walk out to the car park. By day three, Tizer was walking out to the grass and lifting his leg to have a wee. Tizer was then able to go home with his medication, and I asked to see him again two weeks later.

It was amazing. Tizer was completely back to normal – pulling on the lead, and desperate to come and say hello to me. He was such an unusual case and it was such a lovely story – they even wrote an article about it in the local newspaper!

It was nearly three years ago now, and Tizer and is still going strong and full of beans today. He still takes his medication every day, and if we try to stop it, he gets weak again, so it is likely that he will have to stay on the drug for the rest of his life. Tizer's family were very glad that he made such a good recovery, and Tizer gives me lots of fuss and tail wags whenever he visits.

BEING A VET IS QUITE DIFFERENT FROM BEING A DOCTOR

This is mainly because our patients can't tell us what's wrong. The first thing we do as vets is usually take a full history from the owner or keeper of the animal – this means that we ask lots of questions about the animal, what concerns the owner or keeper has and anything else that may be relevant. They can tell us what clinical signs the animal has been showing and for how long. It is important that the vet asks the right types of questions and in the right way to get as much reliable information as possible.

After that we do a physical examination. This is a thorough examination of the animal – and we usually work nose to tail. We look in the ears, mouth, eyes, all over the skin, and we may bend and flex limbs and feel joints. We listen to the heart and lungs and sometimes gut sounds, and we may take the body temperature. These are just some of the things that we do in a basic physical examination.

Sometimes after a taking a history and doing a physical examination we may need to do some more tests. This may involve taking blood samples or using imaging equipment such as an ultrasound machine or an X-ray machine. These machines help us to see inside the body using X-rays or ultrasonic waves.

X-RAYS
IT'S NOT ALWAYS BLACK AND WHITE

A radiograph (which is the image we see) is produced by using X-rays to take a picture of an object. Vets use these images to look at the internal structure of an animal. X-rays don't pass through bone and so the skeleton of an animal looks white, and although X-rays mainly pass through the other internal organs, differences in the thickness of them means that we can quite often see the inside of an animal in some detail.

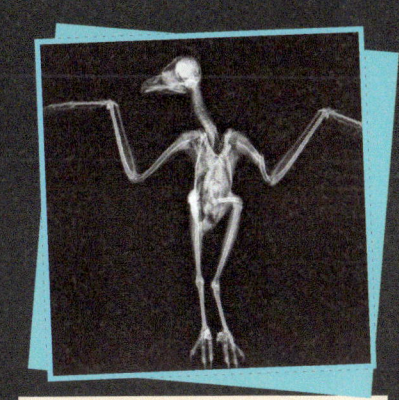

Sometimes we can look at the whole of the animal.

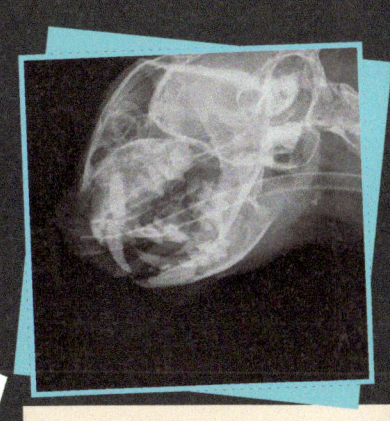

Sometimes we are only looking at one specific bit.

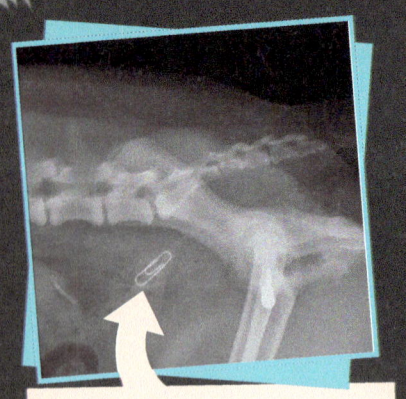

Sometimes we find things we don't expect to find.

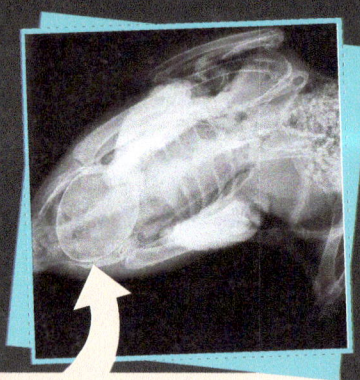

Sometimes we can find exactly what we were looking for

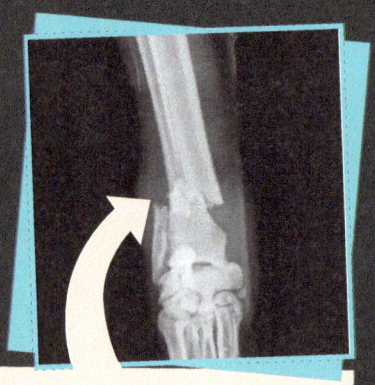

Sometimes the problem can be obvious

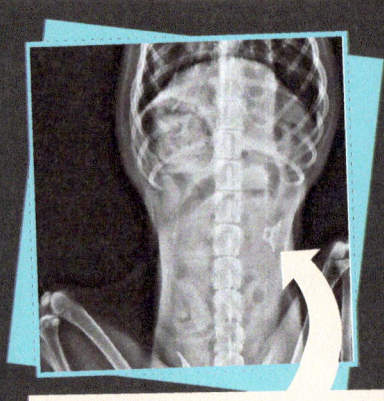

And sometimes it's not so obvious

ULTRASOUND
An ultrasound machine uses ultrasonic waves emitted by a probe to produce an image on a screen. Ultrasound is another good way see what's going on inside an animal. It is especially useful for telling if an animal is pregnant or not.
HOW MANY BABIES CAN YOU SEE?

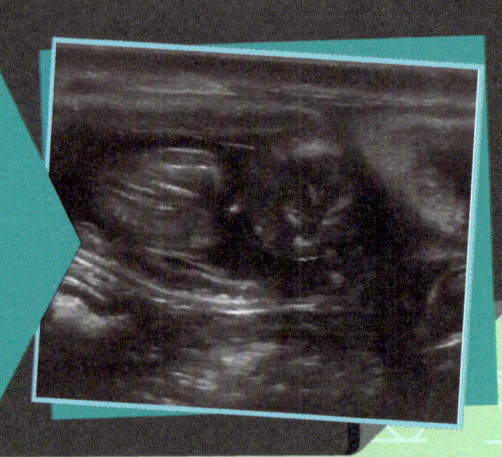

A BUG'S LIFE

A very common reason that dogs, cats and even rabbits and hamsters come to the vet, is for itchy skin. Fleas are the most common culprit of causing itching, but lots of other types of bugs can cause itching and sore skin.

At work I sometimes take skin and hair samples and examine them using a microscope. Here are some of the things that I see:

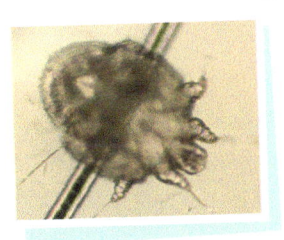

SARCOPTES - this is a type of mite that makes dogs VERY itchy. It's thought that dogs can pick up this mite from being in contact with foxes!

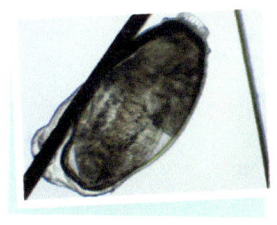

LICE - Lice are just big enough to be seen with the human eye. Lice lay eggs that stick to the hair shaft. It's lice eggs in humans that we refer to as 'nits'.

HARVEST MITES - these mites are related to spiders and cause patches of yellowy-orangey scabbing, usually on the legs of affected dogs. As their name suggest, they are usually picked up outside in woodland or on grassland.

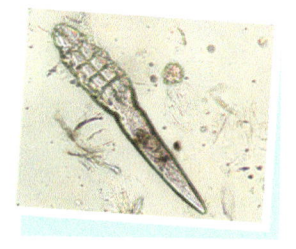

DEMODEX - this strange little mite can sometimes cause a problem in dogs, but can be found just living quietly on skin and not causing a problem at all. 50% of humans have demodex mites living at the base of their eyelashes!

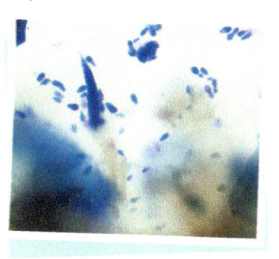

MALASEZZIA - these little footprint-shaped microorganisms are a type of yeast. Low numbers can be found on normal skin - but when they multiply in numbers they can cause significant problems. Dogs with ear disease often have a significant overgrowth of malasezzia which causes inflammation and a brown, waxy discharge in the ears.

TICKS - ticks are little blood suckers and latch onto animals with their mouth parts and get visibly fatter as they enjoy a blood meal. Ticks are an added nuisance as they can spread some quite nasty diseases.

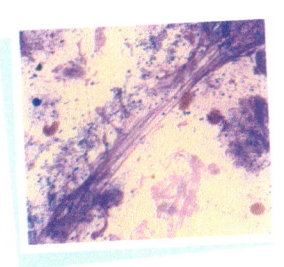

COCCI AND RODS - these are different types of bacteria, defined by their shape. Some types of bacteria are normal inhabitants of the human body and are meant to be there - like those found on the skin surface or in the gut, and these don't cause a problem. Other types of bacteria, or an imbalance of normal bacteria can result in infections.

Once I know what little critter I'm dealing with, I can choose the right treatment to help the pet to get rid of them.

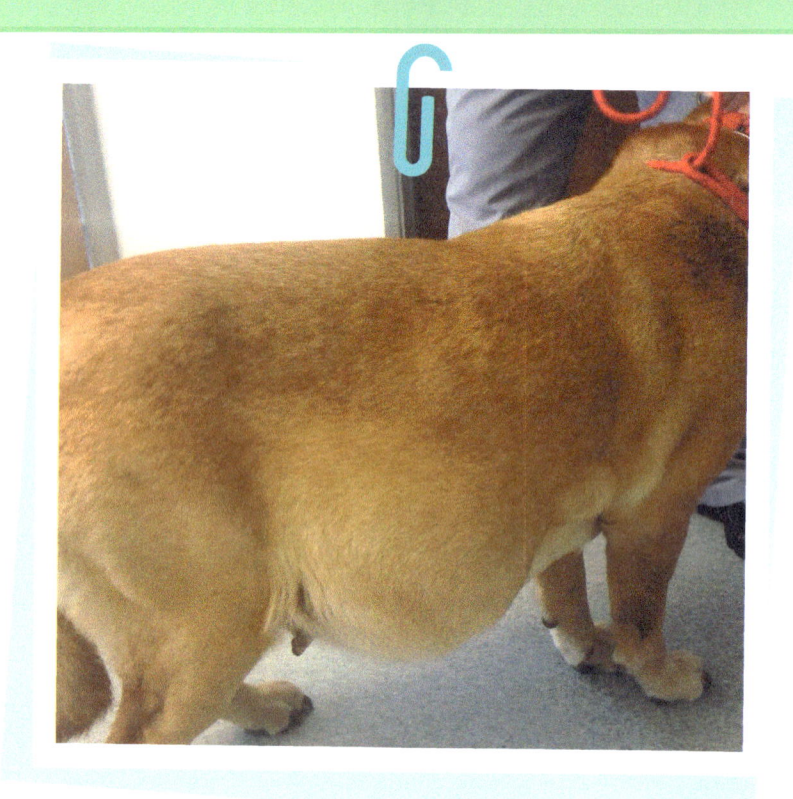

Wilma — a dog with a tumour in her tummy

WILMA WAS A LABRADOR. HER OWNERS BROUGHT HER IN ONE DAY AND THEY WERE VERY UPSET. WILMA HAD A **HUGE** TUMMY – IT WAS QUITE CLEAR THAT SOMETHING WAS WRONG.

Her owners were sure that she had a tumour and were concerned that now it was so large Wilma was getting too uncomfortable and was struggling to move around properly. They had actually brought her in to put her to sleep as they thought that she was suffering, now that the lump had grown so big.

I examined Wilma and agreed that she probably had a tumour. Wilma did have a very big tummy and I could feel a large mass in there – and lots of fluid. However, Wilma had definitely had the huge lump inside her for a while and so I wondered that although it was most likely a type of cancer (tumour), it could be a slow-growing one and not particularly nasty – and if so, if we removed it, we could make Wilma feel much better and she could go back to living a normal life.

> **IT WASN'T WITHOUT RISK. WILMA WAS AN OLDER DOG ANYWAY, AND I COULDN'T BE SURE IF WHAT I THOUGHT ABOUT THE TUMOUR WAS TRUE**

It wasn't without risk. Wilma was an older dog anyway, and I couldn't be sure if what I thought about the tumour was true, but the alternative was grim and so we talked through the procedure to remove the lump in Wilma's abdomen and the owners agreed that I should give it a go.

Wilma had her surgery that day. The vet nurses carefully prepared her for an anaesthetic and we took some X-rays first to check that there was no sign that the cancer had spread. I then made a large hole in Wilma's tummy and removed the mass – which was a tumour the size of a small watermelon – and weighed 4.5 kg! It came away quite easily and after sewing her back up, Wilma recovered well after surgery and went home later that day.

Wilma had a new lease of life after having the lump removed and went back to being playful and energetic, as she had been before she was poorly. Wilma lived for a further two years after the surgery and died of old age.

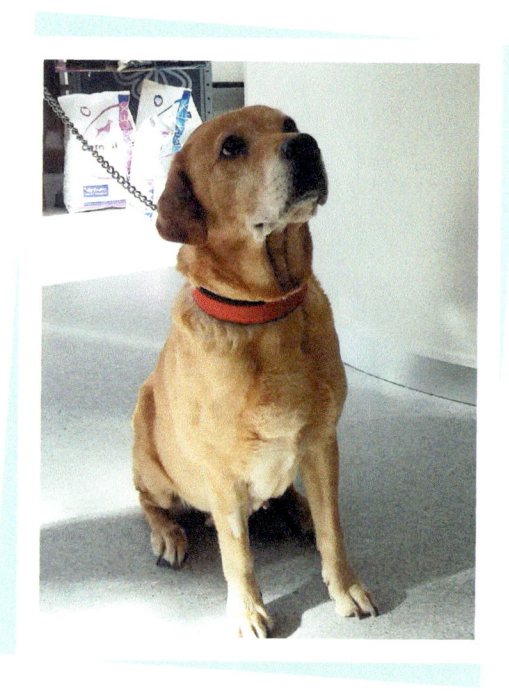

How Cheeto cheated death

THERE IS A SAYING THAT CATS HAVE NINE LIVES. IF THAT IS TRUE THEN CHEETO DEFINITELY ONLY HAS EIGHT LEFT.

Cheeto turned up at home one morning (after being out all night) with one of the worst wounds I have ever seen. The wound was very deep and whatever made the cut must have been extremely sharp. He was a VERY lucky cat, as between the severed muscles I could quite clearly see the huge nerve that runs down the back leg, and running alongside this was a very LARGE blood vessel. If the cut had gone ANY deeper, Cheeto would have damaged this blood vessel, which would have caused extensive bleeding, and it is likely Cheeto would have died.

Luckily Cheeto is a big, strong cat, and after making sure that he had sustained no other injuries, and that his heart and his lungs were all OK, we gave Cheeto a general anaesthetic, flushed and cleaned the wound, and sewed his leg back together. The operation went really well, but even so, I was worried that Cheeto wouldn't regain completely normal function of the injured leg. However, 10 days later Cheeto came back to see us and have his stitches out – walking completely normally – and since that day has never looked back! He is one lucky cat!

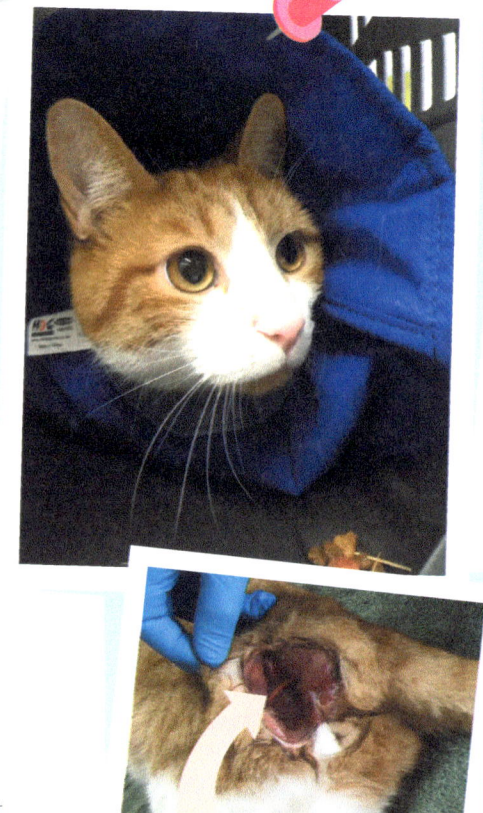

Very important nerve

WE GAVE CHEETO A GENERAL ANAESTHETIC, FLUSHED AND CLEANED THE WOUND, AND SEWED HIS LEG BACK TOGETHER

One-eyed Honey

HONEY IS A GUINEA PIG WHO CAME TO THE VETS WITH A REALLY POORLY EYE.

Honey had suffered some sort of injury to her eye, and it had clouded over. I could see the surface of the eye was damaged, and the eye looked very bulgy and around the edges was really red and sore. Luckily Honey's other eye was OK, and we made the difficult decision to remove Honey's poorly eye – as it was so badly damaged. We knew that we couldn't fix it just using medical treatment such as eye drops and pain relief.

Honey had the operation that day and once she had recovered from the anaesthetic, we could tell she felt much better. Honey continues to live her life with only one eye – but is certainly no worse off for it!

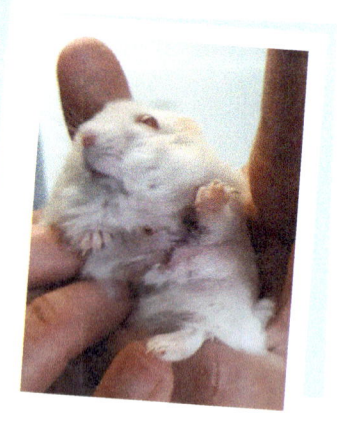

Bernie's big lump

THIS IS BERNIE THE HAMSTER. BERNIE HAD A BIG LUMP UNDER ONE OF HIS FRONT LEGS.

Apart from that, Bernie was fit and healthy, but the lump meant that he was struggling to walk. It was a big lump – about one-quarter the size of Bernie, but feeling around the lump carefully, I was hopeful that we could remove it in full, without causing too much damage to the rest of him. Bernie only weighed 80 g, and generally speaking, the smaller the animal, the greater the risk of an anaesthetic, but after discussing the risk with the owner, they decided Bernie would be much more comfortable without his lump, so we decided to give it a go.

Bernie was placed in a little plexiglass chamber which has tubes going to it carrying anaesthetic gas. After breathing in enough of the gas, Bernie went to sleep and we were able to go ahead with the operation. The operation was a success and we managed to remove Bernie's lump, and he went home later that day with some medicine to make sure he wasn't in pain. He soon made a full recovery and could move around **A LOT** better now that his lump had gone.

7. REACH FOR THE STARS

Finally, we've come to the end of the book. I've given you a whistle-stop tour of the process of applying to vet school, getting into vet school and what life can be like as a vet. There are lots of reasons why you might have read this book, but I imagine for most of you it is because you've thought about what you want to do as a job when you're older, and somewhere on your list of possibilities is being a vet.

I hope this book has provided you with a valuable insight into my job and the profession in which I work, and while it may make some of you reconsider if being a vet is really for you, I expect that many of you will still dream of working with people and animals, or in some alternative role, as a vet when you are older.

I hopefully still have many years left working as a vet, and doing a job that I really enjoy. I have tried to give you a realistic insight into being a vet and have also explored some of the common, and the less commonly chosen career paths that you may choose after you graduate.

Whatever you do in life or as a job, doing something that you love will always bring you greater pleasure than having an easy life or being rich, and research has shown that although being a vet can be hard work and stressful at times, it scores highly when looking at job satisfaction and personal fulfilment. Work hard, aim high and follow your dreams, and remember, never be too proud to ask for help along the way.

I wish you every success in your future, whatever you choose to do, and who knows – if you do end up working as a vet, then maybe I'll see you around!

TO VET SCHOOL AND BEYOND...!